Compact Guide
to Web Page Creation
and Design

Compact Guide to Web Page Creation and Design

Third Edition

Prentice Hall
Information Technology

PEARSON

Prentice
Hall

Upper Saddle River, New Jersey 07458

Editor-in-Chief: Natalie Anderson
Acquisitions Editor: Jodi McPherson
Editorial Assistant: Jodi Bolognese
Manager, Print Production: Christy Mahon
Production Editor & Buyer: Carol O'Rourke
Printer/Binder: Courier, Stoughton

10 9 8 7 6 5 4 3 2
ISBN 0-13-140868-2

Contents

Preface

This book was written to accompany and enhance computer concepts texts by providing practical hands-on instruction on Web page design and creation. Students can use this guide to help them complete lab assignments in which they develop a Web site. The guidelines provided are for creating and publishing Web documents using HTML and JavaScript. They are intended for students who are new to creating Web documents from scratch using HTML. However, because of the inclusion of the introduction to JavaScript, students who are more advanced will also find it useful.

Features of the book include:

♦ Step-by-step instructions with HTML and JavaScript code listings

♦ Instructions on planning a Web document, evaluating the impact of a document, and publishing a document

♦ Screen captures of key instructions

♦ A table of alphabetized HTML tags and attributes used in the book to encourage students to try various options when creating their documents

♦ A Try This! section at the end of every chapter with suggestions for student projects

Overview of Web Publishing

- Browsing the World Wide Web
- Using Browser Software
- Understanding HTML
- Creating Web Pages with an Editor
- Creating Web Pages with HTML
- Planning a Web Page
- Web Page Design Checklist
- ❖ *Plan a Personal Web Page*

This chapter provides an overview of the World Wide Web, browsers, HTML, and introduces the basic principles of designing a web page.

Browsing the World Wide Web

The World Wide Web, also known as the Web or WWW, is the Internet service that has revolutionized communications in the '90s. Prior to the early 1990s university staff, government employees, and military personnel who were doing research or had computer expertise were the only people who used the Internet extensively. Now millions of users are surfing or browsing the Web and even publishing their own Web pages.

In 1989, Tim Berners-Lee at CERN, the European Laboratory for Particle Physics in Geneva, Switzerland, developed a new set of standards for exchanging information on the Internet. The World Wide Web provided a way to link documents on any computer on any network. The release of the World Wide Web in 1992, based on public specifications, has allowed everyone to develop Web pages.

The World Wide Web is a web of documents on servers—computers all over the world. These documents are linked by hypertext. That is, the user clicks on a "hot" spot in the document, and is transferred to the linked document. Hypertext, which is the hot text, contains the address of the computer where the linked document resides and generally appears underlined and in a different color from the surrounding text.

Software, known as a browser, is needed to find and process the hypertext links. The early browsers were text based. In 1993, the National Center for Computing Applications (NCSA) released Mosaic, developed by Marc Andreessen and others at the University of Illinois at Champaign-Urbana. Mosaic was the first graphical Web browser, allowing users to transfer graphics and text. Since the release of the first graphical browser, the Web has become the communications phenomenon of the late 20th century with countless businesses and individuals wanting a presence on the Web.

This linking of any document to any other document allows for nonlinear, non-sequential communications. That is, rather than having to progress through information one page after another as you do with a book, the user browses through the information by clicking on hypertext or hypermedia (which includes video and audio clips) in the document. In this way, the user is able to read the information in any order rather than in a pre-defined order.

The information on the Web resides on host computers known as Web servers. The computer on your desk, from which you access information on the World Wide Web, is known as the client.

The client computer, which is running a browser, requests the linked document. The protocol or standard that enables the transfer of the request and the subsequent transfer of the linked document is HTTP, Hypertext Transfer Protocol.

Linking to any of the millions of Web documents that are on thousands of different servers in thousands of locations requires an addressing scheme. Each network has a unique address and each computer on the network has an address based on the network to which it is connected. The address, based on the Internet Protocol (IP), appears as a long string of numbers separated by periods, for example 198.163.232.254. Because the long numeric IPs are so hard for users to deal with, most networks also have domain names, which are converted into the numeric IP by software. The domain names are words separated by periods, for example:

```
efn.org
```

In this example, org is the top-level domain name (or suffix) and efn is the second-level domain name.

Top-level Domains

The suffix of the domain name specifies the type of organization to which the computer belongs. The global (unsponsored) suffixes are open to be registered by any organization or individual, anywhere in the world. For example, a business in France can register a .com domain, just as easily as a business in the United States, or in Canada. Table 1.1 lists the global suffixes.

TABLE 1.1 GLOBAL SUFFIXES

SUFFIX	TYPE OF ORGANIZATION
.com	Commercial organization
.org	Nonprofit organization
.net	Networks
.biz	Businesses
.info	Organizations offering information
.name	Individuals (wishing to register their name)
.tv	Television and multimedia organizations

Frequently, the domain name also has a suffix that identifies the country in which the server is located. For example, au tells you that the document is located on a server in Australia, as in the address: http://www.freenet.org.au/index.html. These are called country code top-level domains (ccTLD).

Some very small countries have opened up their ccTLD to organizations who might be interested in using it because of its resemblance to real words. For example, the .tv domain suffix technically belongs to the polynesian country of Tuvalu, but they have opened up its registration to any organizations looking to identify themselves on the Web as being related to telelvision (or multimedia, for that matter). The country of Belize has done the same with their .bz domain to attract business-related organizations.

A third category of top-level domains are those that are considered sponsored, either by a government or an industrial association. These domains are far more restricted as to the types of organizations that can register them, though a few are open to organizations worldwide. The more common of these top-level domains (.gov, .edu, etc.) were among the first created by the US government, back in the 1980s; others have been introduced only recently (2000), and are governed by a delegated authority (.aero, for instance, is governed by the SITA: International Association of Aviation Telecommunications). Table 1.2 lists some of the sponsored top-level domains.

TABLE 1.2 SPONSORED SUFFIXES

SUFFIX	TYPE OF ORGANIZATION
.gov	Government (US only)
.mil	Military (US only)
.edu	Educational institution (US only)
.int	Organizations established by international treaties
.aero	Aviation industry members
.coop	Cooperatives
.museum	Museums

When a user requests a document by clicking a link, a Domain Name Server (DNS) matches the domain name with the numeric IP address. Once the address of the Web server is known, the IP protocol checks with the router—a computer on the Internet that finds routes for the packets of information to travel. For this addressing scheme to work, each Web site must have a unique domain name, and somebody must keep track of all the domain names. The Internet Corporation for Assigned Names and Numbers (ICANN) approves unique names and delegates registrars to keep track of the domain names.

The URL

The address of a document, known as its URL—Uniform Resource Locator, appears as the following address for the history of the White House:

http://www.whitehouse.gov/history/life

In this example, http: names the protocol used and tells the browser how to deal with the document. The protocol is usually separated from the second part, the domain name, with two forward slashes (/). The domain name often begins with the three characters www to signify that the document is on a Web server. The last part of the URL (preceded by a single forward slash) is the path or folder on the server where the file is located, and sub-folders may be part of this path.

The name of the desired file is the last part of the URL. If no file name is specified, the URL refers to the default file in that folder. The example just cited tells the browser to use the Hypertext Transfer Protocol (http) to retrieve the document that is located on the host computer (www.whitehouse.gov) in the sub-folder "life" (of the folder "history"), and that the document is a hypertext document (.html). Because the document name in a URL is case sensitive, you must type carefully. Also be sure to include the punctuation exactly, and never include spaces. If you type the example address correctly into your browser address text box, you will be connected to the White House (see figure 1.1).

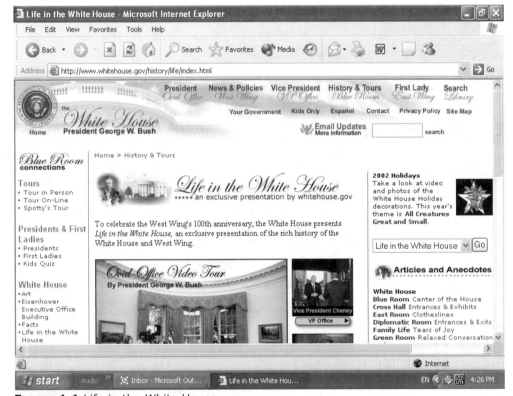

FIGURE 1.1 Life in the White House

The document that appears on the client's screen is called the home page, which is simply the top or first page in a Web document.

Using Browser Software

Your computer must have browser software to access documents on the Web. The Web server transfers the information to the browser, and then the connection is broken. Each request by the client computer requires a new, separate connection to the Web server. Another feature that is unique to browsers is when your browser loads a Web page, it keeps a copy for a limited period of time in a memory location called a cache. When you decide to return to that page, the document may be loaded very quickly if it is loaded from the cache instead of the distant Web server.

There are many different Web browsers available, and it is important to remember that each displays Web documents in a unique way. For example, someone using Internet Explorer will see a Web page displayed differently than someone using Netscape. However, both displays will be similar. Web designers who use style sheets (see Chapter 3, Enhancing the Web Page, on page 31) and who adhere to the current HTML standards should be able to reduce these differences, making it possible to create truly browser-generic Web sites.

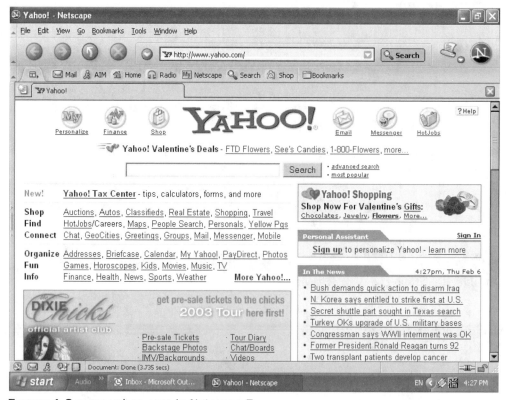

FIGURE 1.2 www.yahoo.com in Netscape 7

All graphical browsers allow you to click on links and then to move back to the previous displayed page or move back to your opening page. Browsers allow you to open files by typing in the correct URL, and they also allow you to print the Web document. Browsers allow you to set bookmarks to mark any page that you want to return to at a later time. Bookmarks are maintained by the browser even after you turn off your computer.

While you are online with the browser loaded, a history list of the last documents that you displayed is maintained. By selecting a site from the history list, you can quickly move to a document directly rather than moving back on Web page at a time. Loading pages with graphics can be slow, and you might want to speed up the process by not loading graphics. You do not have to use a different browser; you simply set your graphical browser to load pages as text only.

Many pages contain forms. Users can complete these forms in order to request more information or to be added to a mailing list. Your browser displays the form, takes the data that is typed into the form and sends it to the appropriate person in the form of an e-mail.

The two most popular browsers today are Netscape Navigator and Microsoft Internet Explorer.

Figure 1.2 shows the Yahoo! Web page, using the Netscape 7 browser to display it.

Figure 1.3 shows Microsoft's home page, using the Internet Explorer 6 browser to display it.

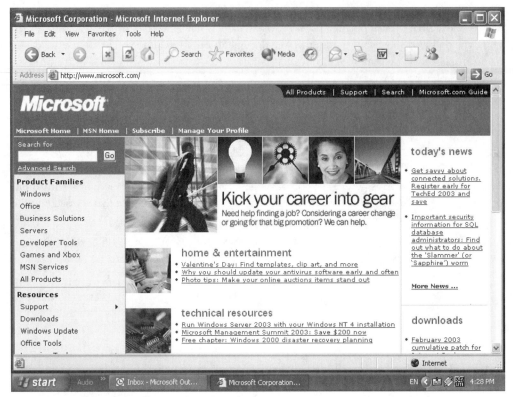

FIGURE 1.3 www.microsoft.com

Understanding HTML

Web pages are made up of text, graphics, and links to other documents. You use HTML (Hypertext Markup Language) to provide browsers with information about how to display pages and create links. HTML is the Web's universal programming language; it's not specific to any platform, computer brand, or operating system. It is a simple markup language that places codes or tags in a Web document, providing information to browsers about the structure of the document.

HTML, developed in 1989, is actually a simplified version of the SGML language (short for Standard Generalized Markup Language), which was developed to share documents on different types of computers. HTML contains one added feature: the use of hypertext to link documents.

The first version of HTML contained only about 30 commands (tags), which the user embedded in a document. The subsequent versions contributed to expanding the capability of the language to the point where highly interactive, dynamic Web sites could be created. The World Wide Web Consortium (W3C) is the international organization dedicated to maintaining and improving the standards used by the World Wide Web, like HTML.

HTML documents are actually text (ASCII) files with HTML tags embedded. HTML tags tell browsers how to display the document; however, each browser interprets the commands in its own way. For example, if you define a line of text on your Web page as a heading, each browser that displays the document knows to display the line of text as a heading. However, each browser might embellish the text in the heading differently, so your Web document will look different when displayed in different browsers.

For any Web page that you display in your browser, you display the HTML by having the browser display the source code. Figure 1.4 displays a Web document, and Figure 1.5 displays the source code.

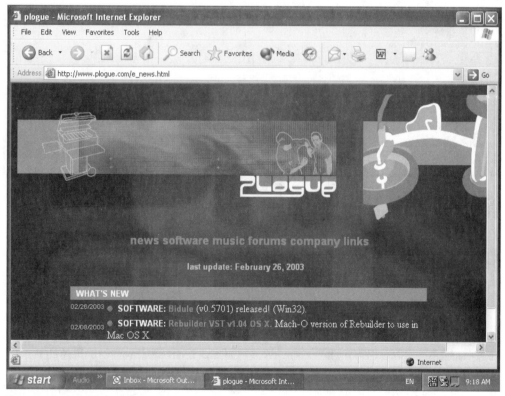

FIGURE 1.4 A Web document

To view the source code in Netscape, choose View>Page Source. To view the source code using Internet Explorer, choose View>Source.

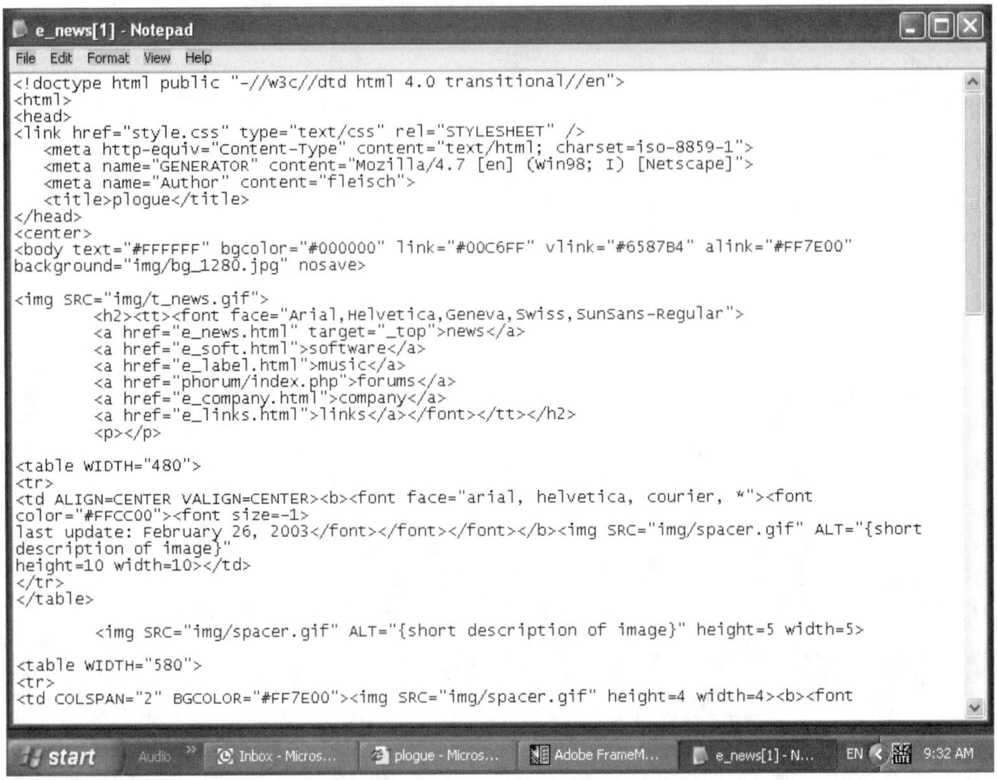


```
<!doctype html public "-//w3c//dtd html 4.0 transitional//en">
<html>
<head>
<link href="style.css" type="text/css" rel="STYLESHEET" />
   <meta http-equiv="Content-Type" content="text/html; charset=iso-8859-1">
   <meta name="GENERATOR" content="Mozilla/4.7 [en] (Win98; I) [Netscape]">
   <meta name="Author" content="fleisch">
   <title>plogue</title>
</head>
<center>
<body text="#FFFFFF" bgcolor="#000000" link="#00C6FF" vlink="#6587B4" alink="#FF7E00"
background="img/bg_1280.jpg" nosave>

<img SRC="img/t_news.gif">
        <h2><tt><font face="Arial,Helvetica,Geneva,Swiss,SunSans-Regular">
        <a href="e_news.html" target="_top">news</a>
        <a href="e_soft.html">software</a>
        <a href="e_label.html">music</a>
        <a href="phorum/index.php">forums</a>
        <a href="e_company.html">company</a>
        <a href="e_links.html">links</a></font></tt></h2>
        <p></p>

<table WIDTH="480">
<tr>
<td ALIGN=CENTER VALIGN=CENTER><b><font face="arial, helvetica, courier, *"><font
color="#FFCC00"><font size=-1>
last update: February 26, 2003</font></font></font></b><img SRC="img/spacer.gif" ALT="{short
description of image}"
height=10 width=10></td>
</tr>
</table>

        <img SRC="img/spacer.gif" ALT="{short description of image}" height=5 width=5>

<table WIDTH="580">
<tr>
<td COLSPAN="2" BGCOLOR="#FF7E00"><img SRC="img/spacer.gif" height=4 width=4><b><font
```

FIGURE 1.5 Source code

Creating Web Pages with an Editor

There are numerous ways to create documents for the World Wide Web. You can use your word processor, such as Microsoft Word 2002 to create a document as you ordinarily would and then choose File>Save as HTML. This option will place all of the HTML tags into your document for you. A second approach that you can use to create Web documents with Word 2002 is to create the Web page using a Microsoft Wizard. Choose File>New>General Templates. Browse to the Web Pages section, and double-click Web Page Wizard. Figure 1.6 shows the one of the Wizard screens.

If you are using Netscape Communicator, you can use Netscape Composer to create your pages. From Navigator, choose Communicator>Page Composer. The Netscape Composer displays, as shown in Figure 1.7.

Using Netscape Composer, you can create a Web document from scratch, use one of the built-in templates, or even get the Page Wizard to help you create your page.

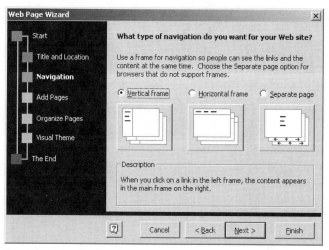

FIGURE 1.6 Word wizard

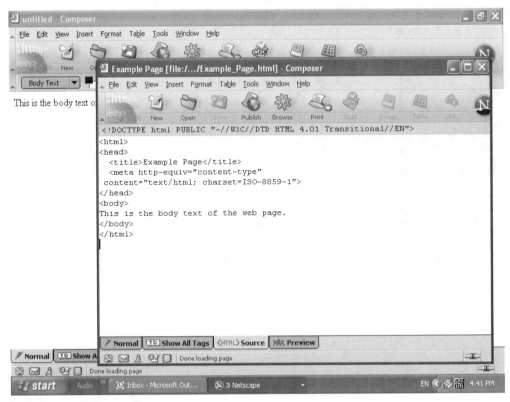

FIGURE 1.7 Netscape Composer

Other Web editors that are popular include Macromedia Dreamweaver, Microsoft FrontPage, Hot-Dog Professional, HotMetal Pro, or WebEdit Professional.

Creating Web Pages with HTML

If you want to build your pages from scratch, you can use Windows Notepad. Simply click the Start menu and choose Programs>Accessories>Notepad. Figure 1.8 shows a file in Notepad with the Save As dialog box displayed.

When you save an HTML document in Notepad, include the extension .html or .htm and change the Save as Type option to All Files (*.*).

No matter what approach you take to creating your Web documents, you will need to be familiar with HTML. As pages become more complex and interactive, you will want to be able to solve problems, tweak appearances, and learn to include new features on your pages. In order to do so, you will need to do more than have a Wizard create a Web document for you.

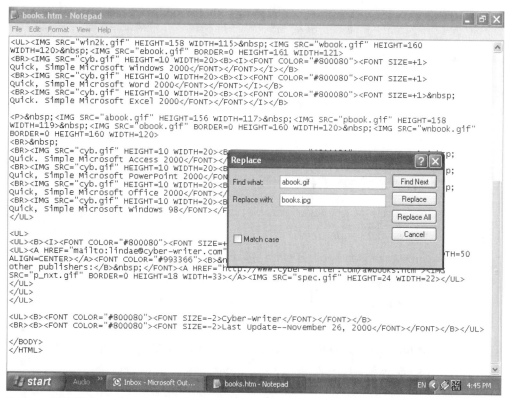

FIGURE 1.8 Notepad

Planning a Web Page

Because anyone can publish on the Web, you will see all kinds of poorly designed, hard-to-read pages. So before you begin creating your Web presentation, you need to do some planning.

To begin designing your Web presentation, answer the following questions:

◆ What is the purpose of this Web presentation?

◆ What audience am I trying to reach and how does that affect my presentation?

◆ What information am I trying to convey?

◆ How will I organize the information?

◆ What should the home or top page have on it to attract visitors?

After defining the goals of your Web presentation, you should define the structure on paper; that is, draw all the pages, define all the links, and make all your decisions before you start to build.

Use the top page or home page to organize the entire site. Create a list that links to all next level pages.

Use a consistent layout for each page in the presentation; that is, use the same background, the same buttons in the same location on each page, and consistent type.

A good rule to remember at this point is to include only one topic per page; keep the pages short enough so that the user does not have to scroll to see the entire page. Do not include a large graphic at the top of the page, as it will take too long to load.

Once you know what you want to say and how you want to present it, you are ready to write the content of the presentation. When writing for online publication, you should follow the guidelines in the Web Page Design Checklist.

Web Page Design Checklist

- ☑ Be brief—use lists whenever possible; use short words in short sentences
- ☑ Be clear—avoid vague words
- ☑ Use simple language—avoid extra words
- ☑ Check your spelling and grammar—the world can visit your site
- ☑ Use the following features to tie the presentation together:

    Use hypertext lists or menus

    Include a link only if it is a useful way to relevant information

    Use consistent terminology throughout the presentation

    Use consistent icons throughout the presentation

    Use the same banner or logo on each page

    Use consistent layout for each page of the presentation

    Include a way back to the home page on each page and place it in the same location on each page

    Make sure all links are current

    Include a graphic only if it relates to the content

    Include alternative text with every graphic

    Make sure each page can stand alone yet remains consistent with the rest of the site

    Don't overdo emphasizing or formatting text

    Make sure the text stands out from the background

    Use lines to separate sections of the page

- ☑ Try out the presentation in more than one browser

❖ TRY THIS!

Plan a Personal Web Page

- ☑ Display a page in your browser. Display the source code.
- ☑ Find Web pages that belong to friends, instructors, or even people you don't know. Get an idea of content that you would want on your Web page.
- ☑ Plan a personal home page. Using the design questions in this chapter, determine the purpose, content, audience, etc. for your Web page.
- ☑ Create a paper design of your proposed Web site.
- ☑ For more information on HTML, visit the World Wide Web Consortium at http://w3.org/

Basic HTML

- Understanding HTML Tags
- Using HTML Structure Tags
- Placing Headings in a Document
- Placing Text in a Document
- Inserting Line Breaks
- Enhancing Text
- Creating Nested Tags
- Using Attributes With Tags
- Creating Lists
- ❖ *Create a Web Page and Include Text*

This chapter describes the basic structures for formatting text in an HTML document.

Understanding HTML Tags

HTML (Hypertext Markup Language) is a set of codes that you use to create a document. These codes, called tags, format text, place graphics on the page, and create links. Because of this, the work of creating a Web page is often referred to as "coding".

These HTML tags follow a certain format, or syntax. Each tag begins with an opening angle bracket (<), ends with a closing angle bracket (>), and contains a command between the brackets; for example, <HTML> is the tag that designates the beginning of an HTML document.

Many of the tags are paired; that is, the first tag indicates the beginning of the command, and the second tag ends the command. The closing tag of the pair has the same syntax as the opening tag, but includes a forward slash (/) before the command. For example, the tag for the ending of an HTML document is </HTML>. All text between the opening and closing tags is affected by the tags. For example:

```
<HTML>
the entire Web document
</HTML>
```

If you forget to close a paired set of tags or you include a backslash or some other character rather than a forward slash, the tag will not be closed, and the command will stay in effect.

Using HTML Structure Tags

A Web page has two main sections: the head section and the body section. The head section must contain a title, and may also contain other information such as formatting styles for the document, or keyword information for Web search engines. Many browsers display this title in the title bar when the document is displayed. The body section contains the information—text, graphics, and so on—that will appear on the screen. The structure of a Web document looks like:

```
<HTML>
    <HEAD>
        <TITLE> text that appears in the browser's title bar</TITLE>
    </HEAD>
    <BODY>
        all information that will be displayed on the screen
    </BODY>
</HTML>
```

Remember these points about titles:

*   A Web page can have only one title.
*   The title should be specific and descriptive because it is displayed as a line item in a browser's history list, in bookmarks, and in indexes or other programs that catalog Web pages.
*   The title should be concise.
*   A title cannot be formatted like other text—you cannot change its appearance.

♦   A title cannot link to other pages.

Placing Headings in a Document

Once you have set up the structure of the Web document, you are ready to place text on the Web page. You can use headings to organize the body of your Web documents, much like an outline organizes a regular document. HTML has six levels of headings, designated by the following tags:

```
Heading 1 <H1>...</H1>
Heading 2 <H2>...</H2>
Heading 3 <H3>...</H3>
Heading 4 <H4>...</H4>
Heading 5 <H5>...</H5>
Heading 6 <H6>...</H6>
```

Heading 1 is the most prominent of the headings and Heading 6 the least prominent. When you use the heading tags, you are telling the browser to format the text as a heading. Each individual browser formats each level of heading its own way, so you are simply setting up a structure for each browser to follow. You will probably use the first three levels most often.

Because the title you place in the <TITLE> tag in the head section of the Web page is displayed only in the title bar of the browser, you should include a title for the page in the body section of the document. To make the title appear as text on the Web page, use the first-level heading to restate the title of the page, or to provide a more complete title. Figure 2.1 shows a sample page with the title in the title bar and the six headings.

One new feature (supported by version 4.0 browsers and higher) is style sheets. This feature works just like the style feature in a word processing program; that is, it applies formatting easily and allows for formatting modifications to be made quickly. You can use style sheets to apply your own formatting to the headings described above. For example, if you want to change the size of the H1 text to 24 point, you would use the <STYLE> tag to redefine the H1 tag. By placing the <STYLE> tag in the <HEAD> section, you would redefine the H1 tag for the entire document. For example:

```
<HTML>
<HEAD>
    <TITLE> title in title bar</TITLE>
    <STYLE type="text/css">
       H1 {font-size: 24pt}
    </STYLE>
</HEAD>
<BODY>
    <H1> Larger heading </H1>
</BODY>
</HTML>
```

Notice the syntax of the <STYLE> tag:

- Always use the attribute TYPE="text/css" to set the style sheet language to CSS. (See page 32 for more information on CSS.)
- Place the name of the tag you want to define right after the open <STYLE> tag.
- Do not place the brackets around the tag to be redefined. Place the new style declarations in curly brackets {....}. A declaration is a definition for a single style attribute.
- The declaration is made up of the property, followed by a colon, and the value to be assigned.
- Close the <STYLE> tag.

Styles are examined in greater detail in chapter 3, page 32.

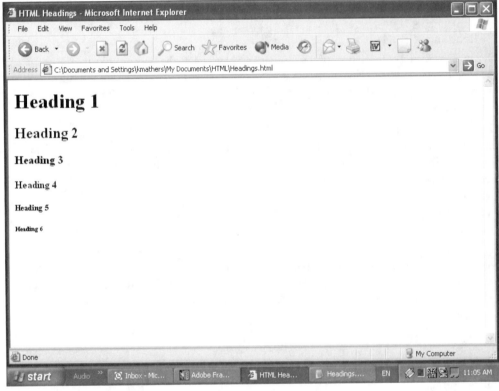

FIGURE 2.1 HTML Headings

Deprecated Elements

The trend in the latest version of HTML (4.01, established in 1999) is to use styles to format text in HTML documents, instead of the headings and tags that are hard-coded into Web browsers. Throughout this book, certain tags and HTML elements are indicated as **deprecated**.

Deprecated elements will eventually be phased out of later revisions of HTML and browsers will stop supporting these features. It is best practice to use the recommended methods for document formatting—your HTML document will have a longer life if you do.

Placing Text in a Document

You are now ready to add text to the HTML document, just as you would in any conventional document. Note that HTML does not recognize when you press the Enter key to end a paragraph. You need to include a <P> tag to start each new paragraph.

Each heading, <H1> through <H6>, automatically includes a paragraph break; therefore, you use the <P> tag only for new paragraphs that don't follow a heading. The end of the paragraph can include the closing paragraph tag </P>, but that's optional. However, you should get into the habit of including it for clarity and completeness. Figure 2.2 shows a sample page in Notepad. Notice the <P> tags.

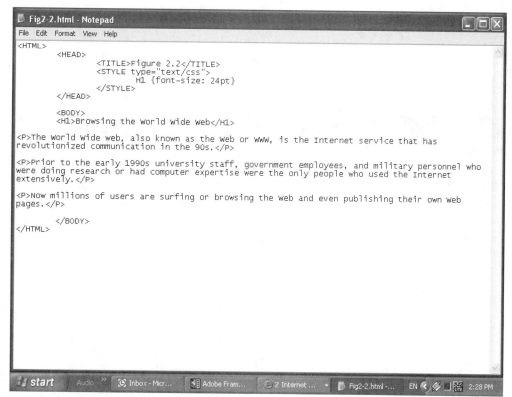

FIGURE 2.2 Codes using <P> tags

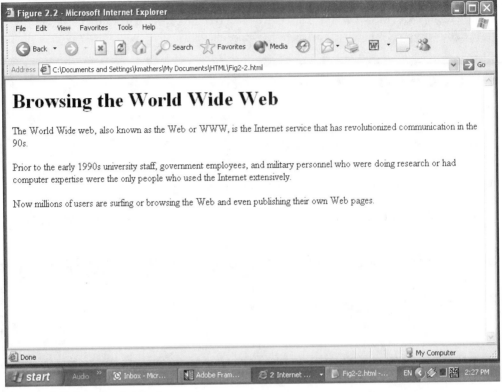

FIGURE 2.3 Result of <P> tags

Figure 2.3 shows the result of those codes displayed in a browser.

Inserting Line Breaks

When you use the paragraph tags (<P>...</P>), browsers insert white space. Sometimes you will want to place some text on a line by itself, without including extra white space above it. You can use the line break tag, <BR>, to place text on the next line. There is no closing tag for the line break tag. Figure 2.4 shows the sample page in Notepad. Notice the <BR> tags. Figure 2.5 shows the results in a browser. Compare the results to Figure 2.3 that used the <P> tags.

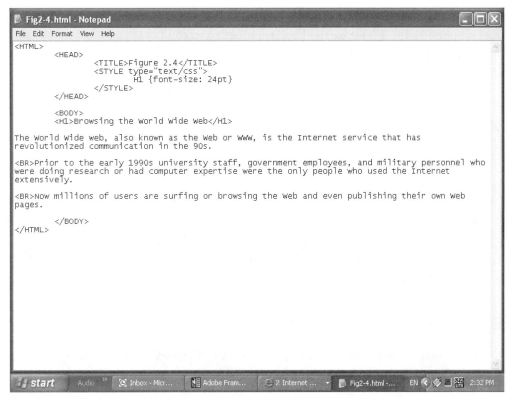

FIGURE 2.4 Code for <BR> tags

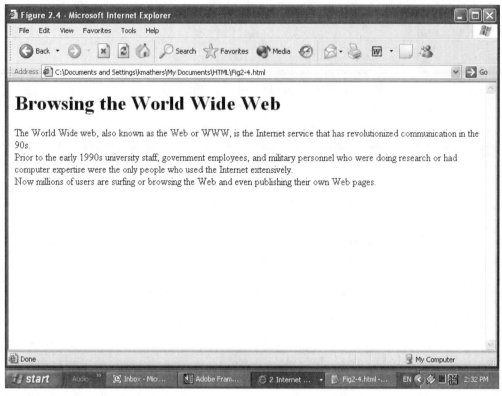

FIGURE 2.5 Result of <BR> tags

Enhancing Text

Emphasizing text by formatting characters is common to all word processing software - you usually select the text and choose the formatting command, such as bold or italic. For the same reasons that you format characters in a word processing document, often you will want to format text in an HTML document. The paired tags <B>...</B>, for example, make the text between the tags bold. This type of formatting is known as physical formatting in Web documents.

The appearance of Web documents is controlled by the browser software that the client uses, which may or may not be able to handle some of the specific physical tags in your HTML document.

The second type of formatting, called logical formatting, is the more popular choice. Logical formatting is used more often than physical formatting to get around this problem of browsers not recognizing physical tag and, thus, not formatting the text at all.

Logical formatting tells the browser how the text is to be used. When you use logical formatting tags to format text, you are simply telling the browser to emphasize the text, for example, rather than boldfacing it physically. That way, each browser will give the text some formatting that emphasizes that text. Table 2.1 shows the logical tags, and table 2.2 shows the physical tags.

Remember to use logical tags instead of physical tag whenever possible. Also remember that too much formatting makes the screen hard to read.

TABLE 2.1 LOGICAL TAGS

TAG	RESULT
<EM> ... </EM>	Emphasis tag, many browsers place the text within the tags in italics.
<STRONG> ... </STRONG>	Provides strong emphasis. Many browsers boldface the text with the tags.
<DEL> ... </DEL>	Indicates that the text (from a previous version) was deleted from the current version of the document. Many browsers render this text with strikes through it.
<INS> ... </INS>	Indicates that the text is new to this version of the document (and replaces the older text, as marked by the <DEL> tag). Many browsers render this text as underlined.

TABLE 2.2 PHYSICAL TAGS

TAG	RESULT
<B> ... </B>	Bolds text
<I> ... </I>	Italicizes text
<CENTER> ... </CENTER>*	Centers text
<U> ... </U>*	Underlines text
<STRIKE> ... </STRIKE>*	Strikes through text
_{...}	Subscripts text—lowers the marked text below the rest of the line. E.g., H_2O
^{...}	Superscripts text—raises the marked text above the rest of the line. E.g., 2^3

NOTE: The tags indicated by the * (<CENTER>, <U>, and <STRIKE>) are considered deprecated in HTML version 4.01, and you should avoid using them whenever possible.

There are various reasons for these deprecations:

- The underline tag can easily be mistaken by the reader for a hypertext link (see chapter 4, Inserting Links on page 48).

- The underline and strike-through physical tags are most often used to indicate deleted and inserted text (for document revisions). The two corresponding logical tags are far better choices for indicating edits of that type. If you need to indicate underlined text in a document, use the <INS> tag, and use <DEL> for strike-through text.

- Alignment, like centering text, is better applied using style sheets instead of individual tags (see chapter 3, page 32 for more information on using styles).

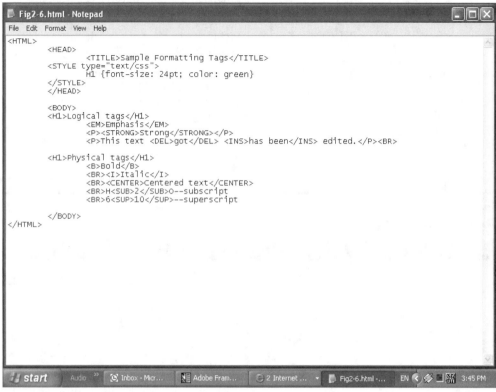

FIGURE 2.6 Codes for text formatting tags

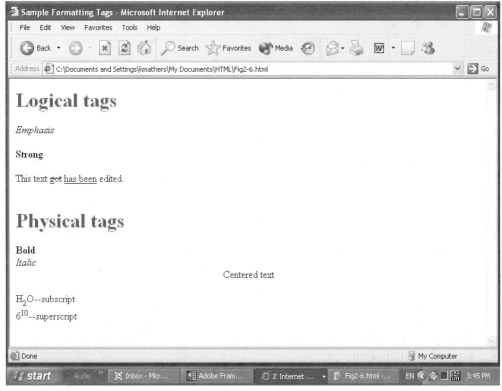

FIGURE 2.7 Result of formatting tags

Creating Nested Tags

Sometimes you may want text to have more than one formatting tag. For example, you may want to insert text and emphasize it. Tags combined in this way are called nested tags. If you want italicized text to be bolded, for example, you would include the <B> tag with the <I> tag.

To make the name Querkus appear as bold and italics, you would write the code as follows:

```
The band's name is <B><I>Querkus</I></B>
```

When you nest tags, pay careful attention to the order in which they are closed. The last tag opened must be closed first. Notice that the italic tag is closed before the bold tag in the example. This is the correct syntax.

Using Attributes With Tags

You can include attributes with tags; these attributes further define the tag. The attribute is entered after the command before the final angle bracket, and is always enclosed in quotation marks.

NOTE: The use of attributes in tags within the Body of an HTML document is deprecated. In HTML 4.01, any changes to the formatting of tags should be set out in the document's style sheet, at the beginning of the document. However, HTML 4.01 does still support this older way of formatting, so in this chapter and the next, deprecated examples of formatting will be included so that you can learn to recognize them in older HTML source code.

With this deprecated type of formatting, some attributes appear by themselves, and other attributes can appear with a value modifier. The syntax of an attribute with a value modifier is as follows: attribute="value".

For example, you could include the ALIGN attribute with an H1 tag to center the heading.

```
<H1 ALIGN="CENTER">Computer Textbooks</H1>
```

In this example, the text Computer Textbooks will appear formatted for Heading 1 because of the <H1> tag and centered because the ALIGN attribute is assigned the value CENTER.

The CENTER value is a given value; that is, you choose one value from the available ALIGN values of LEFT, RIGHT, CENTER. You can choose only one value and no other values are accepted.

Some commands allow you to include an attribute that has any value, for example, a number to define a size or a URL to define an address. Remember all values always need to be enclosed in straight quotation marks ("...").

Creating Lists

Because the text on Web pages needs to be short and concise, placing text in lists can be helpful. The most common type of list is the unordered list (also called a bulleted list). It is a short list of information that does not need to be presented in any particular order. The unordered list appears with bullets (special characters) before each line item.

Remember these important points about unordered lists:

- Each list begins with the <UL> tag and ends with the </UL> tag
- Each line of the list must be indicated with the <LI> tag, which is not paired
- Each line of the list appears indented and is preceded by a bullet (the way the bullet is displayed varies from browser to browser)

Here is an example of an unordered list:

```
<UL>
    <LI>first item
    <LI>second item
    <LI>third item
</UL>
```

Sometimes the information you are presenting in a list should be in a defined sequence, such as instructions for steps in a process. You can create an ordered list (also called a numbered list). Start the list with the <OL> tag and end the list with the </OL> tag. Within those tags, begin each line you would like numbered with the <LI> tag; the ordered list is automatically numbered for you. Following is an example of an ordered list:

```
<OL>
    <LI>first item
    <LI>second item
    <LI>third item
</OL>
```

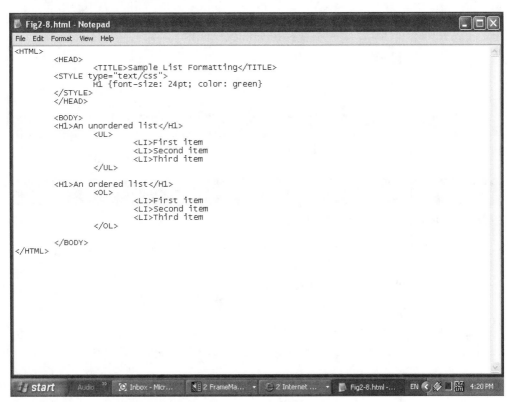

FIGURE 2.8 Code for unordered and ordered lists

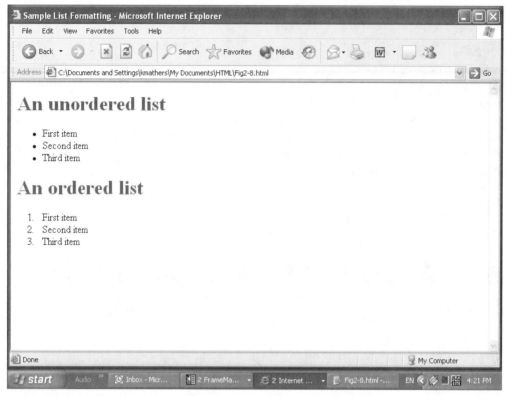

FIGURE 2.9 Results of unordered and ordered lists

❖ TRY THIS!

Create a Web Page and Include Text

☑ Using the design you created in the previous chapter, create the structure for your Web page.

☑ Include text on the Web page.

☑ Include an unordered list.

☑ Format the headings using styles.

☑ Format the text using logical and physical tags.

Enhancing the Web Page

- Formatting with Cascading Style Sheets
- Adding a Horizontal Line
- Including Graphics
- Adding a Background Color
- Using a Graphic as a Background
- Changing Text Color
- Using Special Characters
- Inline Styles
- Including Tables
- ❖ *Enhance Your Web Page*

This chapter describes the basic design code used to enhance the visual presentation of Web pages.

Formatting with Cascading Style Sheets

As mentioned in chapter 2, **styles** are ways of predefining formatting so that formatting changes can be applied to the document quickly and easily. Styles also make it easier to make global formatting changes across an HTML document. Because all styles are defined in one place (usually the HEAD section), you only need to make a change in that one place to have it instantly reflected throughout the document.

One of the more common ways of creating styles in an HTML document is by using Cascading Styles Sheets (CSS). This type of style is called "cascading" because more than one style sheet can be applied to the same document. This book assumes that there is only one style sheet in the document.

In a nutshell, a style is used to predefine the format for any HTML tag in the document. For example, if you wanted all the paragraphs of the Body text to be centered, you would use the following code:

```
<HTML>
    <HEAD>
        <TITLE>Document title</TITLE>
        <STYLE type="text/css">
            Body {text-align: center}
        </STYLE>
        </HEAD>
    <BODY>
        <P>Document text (which is centered)</P>
    </BODY>
</HTML>
```

While the style tag does not always have to go in the Head section of your HTML document, it is considered best practice to place all your style definitions there.

The advantage to predefining styles is that you can create many different styles for the same tag, and apply each separately as needed. You do this by defining a **class** for each different style of tag. The class is then used in two places. First, in the style definition:

```
<STYLE type="text/css">
    P {font-style: normal}
    P.ital {font-style: italique}
    P.caps {font-variant: small-caps}
</STYLE>
```

Note that each class of the P tag is identified by placing a period after the tag name and naming the class.

The class is then applied in the Body text of the HTML page by declaring the "class" attribute:

```
<P class = "ital"> This text will be in italics. </P>
<P> This text will not.</P>
```

Remember that the value of any attribute defined within a tag always has to be enclosed in quotation marks.

For example, to have three different styles of paragraph text, you could enter the following:

```
<HTML>
    <HEAD>
        <TITLE>Using Classes</TITLE>
        <STYLE type="text/css">
            P {font-style: normal; font-size: large}
            P.ital {font-style: italique; font-size: large}
            P.caps {font-variant: small-caps; font-size: large}
        </STYLE>
    </HEAD>
    <BODY>
        <P>Document text (which is normal)</P>
        <P class = "ital"> This text will be in italics. </P>
        <P> This text will not.</P>
        <P class = "caps"> Always remember to close your tags! </P>
    </BODY>
</HTML>
```

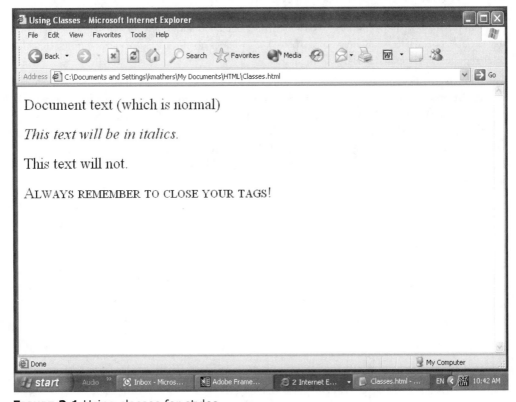

FIGURE 3.1 Using classes for styles

Establishing the two classes means that any text bearing just the <P> tag will look normal, while entire paragraphs can be put in italics simply by adding the text calling the class. Figure 3.1 demonstrates the results in a Web broswer.

It is often advantageous to use predefined classes for variants of tags, instead of physical tags because:

♦ It's easy to forget to close physical tags, while when using a class, simply closing the original tag ends the formatting.

♦ You define the names for the classes, making them easier to remember and more intuitive to apply.

Style sheet definitions do not always have to be stored "inline"; that is, in the HTML document itself. It is also possible (and very efficient) to create a list of style definitions and save it in a separate text file. See chapter 4, Linking External Style Sheets on page 52 for more details.

Adding a Horizontal Line

You can place a horizontal line or "rule" across the page by including the <HR> tag wherever the line should appear. The <HR> tag is not a paired tag; there is no closing tag. You can define HR styles to change the the length and width of the line.

Lines are an effective means of dividing a page. For example, you can use a line to separate the main part of the page from footer information. Footer information should include the author or person responsible for the page, an email address, and other contact information such as a mail address or phone number. The date of the last revision of page is also usually contained in the footer. You can use the <ADDRESS>...</ADDRESS> tag to format the text (usually italic and a reduced font size), or you can format the text yourself. Figure 3.2 shows the code for a line that separates the footer information from the rest of the body, and Figure 3.3 displays the results.

FIGURE 3.2 Code for a footer

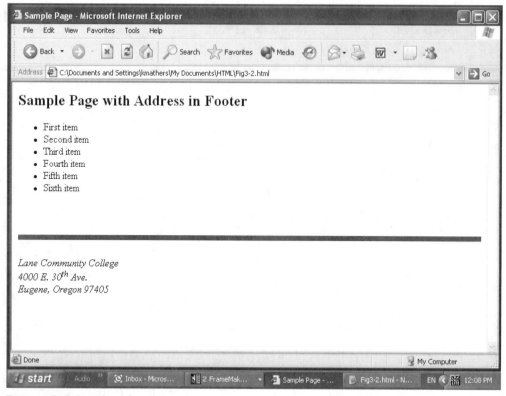

FIGURE 3.3 Results of code

Including Graphics

Two universal formats are used for Web graphics: .GIF and .JPG. The .GIF standard, short for Graphics Interchange Format, was developed by CompuServe and is the format that displays in the greatest number of browsers. The .JPG, which stands for Joint Photographic Experts Group, is best used for images such as photographs that contain many subtle colors.

To include an image on your Web page, you use the <IMG> tag. The tag includes the SRC="filename" attribute. For example, to display a graphic named logo.gif, you enter the following:

```
<IMG SRC="logo.gif">
```

In this example, the image logo.gif will display at the location of the tag.

Including alternative text with images for users who can not or do not want to view images is also a good idea. If a user has graphic display turned off or is using a text browser, the text will be displayed on the person's screen. Alternative text is also used by text-to-speech browsers that aid the visually impaired when accessing the Web.

The syntax for including alternative text is:

```
<IMG SRC="logo.gif" ALT="our company logo">
```

Two other attributes that you should include with every image style are HEIGHT and WIDTH. If you designate a width and height for each image, your page will load into browsers more quickly. The reason for this is that browsers have to calculate the width and height for every image, so by specifying the size, you avoid the calculations. The syntax for including the width and height is:

```
<IMG SRC="logo.gif" ALT="our company logo" WIDTH="40"
HEIGHT="200" >
```

The images are measured in pixels, that is, picture elements. Pixels are dots on your screen that make up the image.

In HTML 4.01, use of the WIDTH and HEIGHT attributes in each instance of the IMG tag is considered deprecated. It is better instead to define styles for the <IMG> tag using classes for each image size.

For instance, the code to resize the same image would look like this:

```
<STYLE type="text/css">
    IMG.logo {width: 40; height: 200}
</STYLE>
....
<IMG SRC="logo.gif" class="logo" ALT="our company logo">
```

Another property to consider adding to the style defntinon for an image is the placement of the image in relation to the surrounding text. This is done by settng the "float". For example, an image with the float set to left would have all text in the same paragraph flow down the right side of the image. The syntax for this is:

```
<STYLE type="text/css">
    IMG.logo {width: 40; height: 200; float: left}
</STYLE>
```

An inline image will always use the same alignment as the text paragraph it is placed in.

You have seen how to create a bulleted list using the <UL> tag. Many people prefer to create or download bullets from clipart sites to enhance their Web page. Once you have a bullet that you want to use, simply type the text, and include the <IMG SRC="bullet.gif"> command where you want the bullet to appear. You can use the same bullet for the entire list or you can use different ones.

You have also used the <HR> tag to create a separator line on a Web page. Many people prefer to create or download color lines from clipart sites to match their bullets and create a more unified look to their pages.

Figure 3.4 shows the code for a logo, bullets, and a line, and Figure 3.5 displays the results.

```
duckweb.html - Notepad
File  Edit  Format  View  Help
<HTML>    <HEAD>
                <TITLE>Welcome To DuckWeb</TITLE>
                <STYLE type="text/css">
                     P {font-family: Arial}
                     P.center {font-family: Arial; text-align: center}
                     IMG.left {float: left}
                </STYLE>
        </HEAD>
        <BODY>
        <P class="center"><IMG SRC="uotitle.gif" ALT="Welcome To DuckWeb"></P>

        <IMG class="left" SRC="duckweb.gif" ALT="Welcome To DuckWeb">
<P>DuckWeb is an interactive web application that provides easy access to
information.  Be prepared to supply your nine-digit User Id and your
Personal Access Code(PAC).  If you are a student, this is the <B>same</B>
PAC you use to access DuckCall.</P>
<P>For security reasons, DuckWeb requires that your browser be configured to
accept cookies. For best performance, it is recommended that you use the 4.x
versions (or later) of Netscape or Internet Explorer.</P>
<P>DuckWeb is generally available 24 hours a day.  There may be occasional
breaks in service when the system is down for routine maintenance,
especially most Friday evenings from 6pm to midnight.</P>

        <BR><BR>
        <IMG class="left" SRC="caution.gif">
        <P><B>REMEMBER</B>, especially if you are using a public terminal, to press the
        <B>LOG OFF</B> button when you are finished.  Avoid using the forward/back buttons on
your browser unless specifically directed to.</P>

        <BR><HR>
        <P class="center"><B>Student Related Links</B>
        <BR><UL>
        <LI>[<a HREF="http://www.uoregon.edu">UO Home Page</a>]
        <LI>[<a HREF="http://duckhunt.uoregon.edu">DuckHunt</a>]
        <LI>[<a HREF="http://registrar.uoregon.edu">Registrar</a>]
        <LI>[<a HREF="http://financialaid.uoregon.edu">Financial Aid</a>]
        </UL></BODY>
</HTML>
```

```
start      Audio  »   Inbox - Micr...   Adobe Fra...    2 Internet...   duckweb.ht...   EN    4:12 PM
```

FIGURE 3.4 Code for logo, bullets, and a line

Adding a Background Color

When you started your Web document, you defined the opening of the body of the document with the <BODY> tag. If you want to change the background color of your Web document from the standard gray, you do so by adding a style for the body tag with the background-color property set. For example, if you want to have a blue background, here is how you do it:

```
<STYLE type="text/css">
    BODY {background-color: #0000FF}
</STYLE>
```

In this example, 00000FF is the RGB (Red, Green, Blue) value of blue; that is, its red, green, and blue values. The first two digits in this number designate the red value; the second two digits, the green value; and the last two digits, the blue value. To specify these RGB values for the color you want, you must know or look up the hexadecimal equivalent that represents the color. Table 3.1 lists some common colors you might want to use.

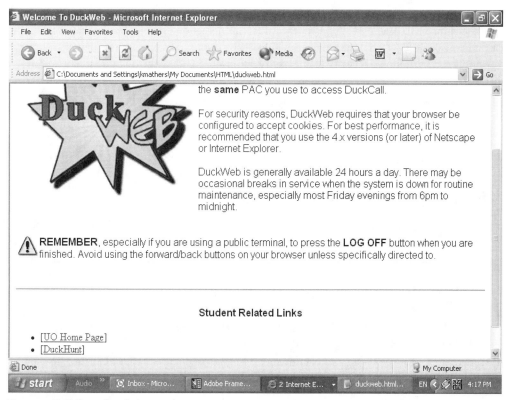

FIGURE 3.5 Result of the code

TABLE 3.1 COMMON COLORS

COLOR	HEX EQUIVALENT
Black	#000000
White	#FFFFFF
Green	#00FF00
Red	#FF0000
Tan	#DEB887
Turquoise	#19CCDF
Magenta	#FF00FF
Yellow	#FFFF00

Hexadecimal (or hex) is a numbering system that uses base 16 rather than base 10. The hex system uses the numbers 0 - 9 along with the letters A - F. This numbering system enables you to represent all numbers up to 256 with only two digits and has been used extensively with computers for that reason. If you are not used to working in hex, do not be confused by the mixture of letters and numbers. Just remember that letters represent numbers greater than 9 with F being the highest.

Using a style to define the body background color is the best way to define the background. That said, many Web sites still use the old way (and Web browsers still understand it), so you should at least learn to recognize the deprecated method of setting the background color:

```
<BODY BGCOLOR = "#0000FF">
```

Using a Graphic as a Background

Instead of changing the background color, you can use an image as the background, such as the company's or organization's logo. To add an image to the background of your Web document, you use the background-image property in the BODY tag style definition. The syntax for this property is:

```
<STYLE type="text/css">
    BODY {background-image: url(logo.gif)}
</STYLE>
```

If the image is small, the browser tiles or repeats the image so that it covers the document's background.

Be sure to use a light colored image that does not make the page difficult to read. Figure 3.6 shows a Web page with a tiled graphic included as a background.

FIGURE 3.6 Page with a tiled graphic for a background

Changing Text Color

After changing the appearance of the paragraphs of a Web document, you might also want to change the color of the text that appears on the page. You do so by adding color rules to the styles defined in your style sheet at the beginning of the document.

You can change the color of four different types of text:

* Change the color of any tag's text (e.g., <P>, <BODY>, <H1>, <H2>, etc.)
* Change the color of links (hypertext) with the A:link selector
* Change the color of visited links (links the user has clicked) with the A:visited selector
* Change the color of active links with the A:active selector. This selector designates the color of the link as you click it.

You use the same RGB hexadecimal equivalents described for the background colors to designate the desired colors of text. To change the body text to red, for example, you would type the following in your style definitions:

```
<STYLE type="text/css">
    BODY {color: #FF0000}
</STYLE>
```

When you use the color property to designate red text with the blue background, it looks like this:

```
<STYLE type="text/css">
    BODY {color: #FF0000; background-color:#0000FF}
</STYLE>
```

These commands designate the (unvisited) links value as pink and the visited links as green.

```
<STYLE type="text/css">
    BODY {color: #FF0000; background-color:#0000FF}
    A:link {color:#F33E96}
    A:visited {color:#00FF7F}
</STYLE>
```

The text below is the deprecated syntax for representing the same formatting:

```
<BODY BGCOLOR=#0000FF TEXT=#FF0000 LINK=#F33E96 VLINK=#00FF7F>
```

Using Special Characters

HTML documents are ASCII text files; that is, they are files based on the American Standard Code for Information Interchange (ASCII). ASCII files use only the letters, numbers, and symbols that you can type from your keyboard, which, along with some essential control characters, equals 128 characters. Just as you might include special characters that are not on the keyboard in a word processing document, you can also include special characters in a Web document. Most word processing software enables you to select the character in a dialog box and insert it into the document. However, to insert special characters using HTML, you need to do so manually—by typing the name or number of the special character.

You can use two methods to include a character from the extended ASCII. If the special character has a name, you can use the name; otherwise, you need to use the character's number, which is designated by its location in the character set. Whether you use the character's name or number, you must start the code with an ampersand (&) and close it with a semicolon (;). The number sign appears immediately after the ampersand in codes using numbers. Table 3.2 shows the syntax for some commonly used special characters.

TABLE 3.2 COMMONLY USED SPECIAL CHARACTERS

CHARACTER	NAME	CODE
©	&copy;	&#169;
®	&reg;	&#174;
È	&Egrave;	&#200;
¥	&yen;	&#165;
£	&pound;	&#163;
>	&gt;	&#62;
<	&lt;	&#60;
&	&amp;	&#38;

Notice that the table includes some characters that are located on your keyboard. These special characters present a problem in HTML because of the syntax of the language. For example, to type A < B, you need to designate the lesser than sign (<) as a special character because a browser interprets all lesser than signs as the start of an HTML tag. The same holds true for other HTML characters.

Inline Styles

While most of the time it is preferable to use a single style definition to handle formatting, there can be times when you need to make a single exception to a specific tag. In those cases, you can define the inline style using the STYLE attribute.

For example, the following code demonstrates how to change the size of only certain characters in a title:

```
<H1><B style="font-size: 38pt">L</B>inks and <B style="font-size:
38pt">R</B>esearch</H1>
```

The text rendered from the example above will look like this:

*L*inks and *R*esearch

When using an inline style, you set the syle definitions the same way you would in the STYLE tag (using CSS language). Still, if you think that there is any chance you might use a particular style more than once, you should always define a class for the tag. Even if you only have one instance of a style in your current version of the document, you may add more instances at a later revision.

Including Tables

Tables are often used in Web page development to display information because you can organize bodies of information so that the reader can quickly see the overall picture.

Tables are made up of data arranged in columns (vertically) and rows (horizontally). The intersection of a column and row is known as a cell; data is placed in cells. Tables can also be used as a design element in HTML. You will find that many people use tables to have control of the elements on the screen.

The entire contents of the table are contained between the opening and closing <TABLE> tags.

```
<TABLE>
entire contents of table
</TABLE>
```

The table is defined row by row; that is, you define the contents of the first row and then the contents of each subsequent row. You start each row with the <TR> tag, which stands for table row, and end each row with the </TR> tag. Everything between those two tags will appear in one row of the table.

The syntax is:

```
<TABLE>
   <TR>
      text in the first row
   </TR>
   <TR>
      text in the second row
   </TR>
   <TR>
      text in the third row
   </TR>
</TABLE>
```

You then define the contents of each cell in each row:

The <TH> tag (table header) is used to bold cell contents, and the <TD> tag (table data) is used for unformatted cells. Both tags are paired tags.

For example, if the first row of a three-column, three-row table contains headings and the rest of the table contains data, this is how the coding looks.

```
<TABLE>
   <TR>
      <TH>heading </TH>
      <TH>heading </TH>
      <TH>heading </TH>
   </TR>
   <TR>
      <TD>data</TD>
      <TD>data</TD>
      <TD>data</TD>
```

```
      </TR>
      <TR>
         <TD>data</TD>
         <TD>data</TD>
         <TD>data</TD>
      </TR>
   </TABLE>
```

Figue 3.7 displays what this code looks like when rendered by the Web browser.

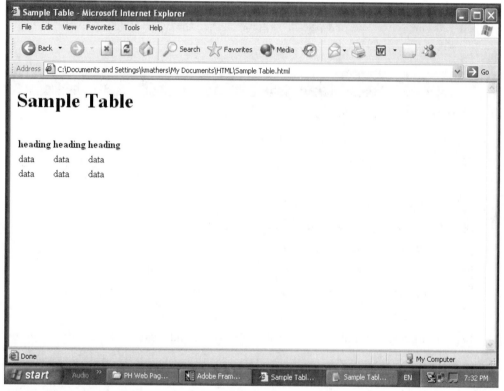

FIGURE 3.7 Sample table

To set a table off from the rest of the Web document, you can add the BORDER attribute to the opening <TABLE> tag. The BORDER attribute places a border with a width of 1 pixel around the outside edge of the table and also places borders around each individual cell. The syntax for the BORDER attribute is:

```
   <TABLE BORDER>
```

To change the width of the outside border, you can add a value to the BORDER attribute. The value is the number of pixels that will appear around the outside edge of the table. To increase the border to a width of 4 pixels, for example, use the format:

```
<TABLE BORDER=4>
```

To change the spacing between cells so that the data is easier to read, you can add the CELLSPACING attribute to the opening <TABLE> tag, along with a value in pixels. The default call spacing is 2 pixels. The following command assigns a value of 8 pixels:

```
<TABLE CELLSPACING=8>
```

To add space around the cell contents, you use the CELL-PADDING attribute along with a value in pixels. The default cell padding is 1 pixel. This command sets the cell padding at 6 pixels:

```
<TABLE CELLPADDING=6>
```

❖ TRY THIS!

Enhance Your Web Page

Enhance your Web page by adding the following:

- ☑ Create style definitions to change the color of the body text, and at least two <P> classes
- ☑ Include a line using the <HR> tag
- ☑ Include a line that you download from a clipart site
- ☑ Include a graphic on the page
- ☑ Include a list with bullets that you download from a clipart site
- ☑ Change the color of the background or include an image on the background
- ☑ Place some information in a table
- ☑ Create a footer that uses the <ADDRESS> tag and includes the copyright symbol

Linking to Other Documents and Creating Forms

- Inserting Links
- Linking Within the Same Document
- Using Graphics and Buttons as Links
- Creating an Email Link
- Linking External Style Sheets
- Creating a Form

❖ *Link Your Documents to Others*

This chapter describes how to use links and forms in your HTML documents. This includes linking to external files, linking within your page, linking a style sheet, and creating a form to send an e-mail with user-submitted information.

Inserting Links

One feature that makes Web documents so powerful is their linking capability. A link provides text or an object that the user can click, and the user's display automatically "jumps" to the new document. The link can be a location within the same document or to a different Web document.

To create a link, use the <A> tag—anchor tag. You set the opening and closing <A> tags around the text that you want the user to click to view another document. The <A> tag must contain the URL (Uniform Resource Locator) for the desired document. The syntax is as follows:

```
<A HREF="URL">text user clicks</A>
```

A more complete URL would look like the following:

```
<A HREF="http://web.site.com/path/document.html">text user
clicks</A>
```

For example,

```
<A HREF="http://prenhall.com">Prentice Hall</A>
```

The text located between the opening and closing <A> tags appears in the browser as hypertext.

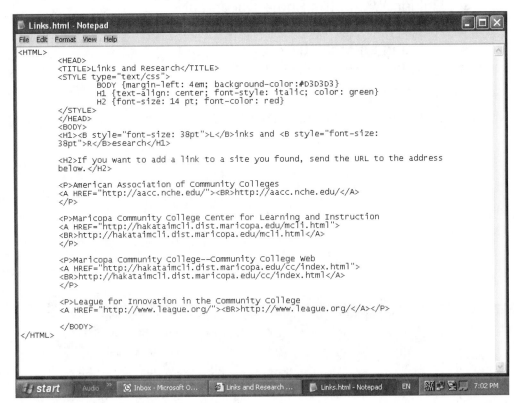

FIGURE 4.1 Code for links

When the user clicks the hypertext, he is transferred to the Web document defined in the URL by the Hypertext Reference (HREF).

You may have seen Web pages that have phrases such as "click here" to indicate a link. The user knows to click the text without having to be told to click there, because the text has been formatted as hypertext—usually blue and underlined. Figure 4.1 shows the code for a page with several links, and Figure 4.2 shows the result in the browser.

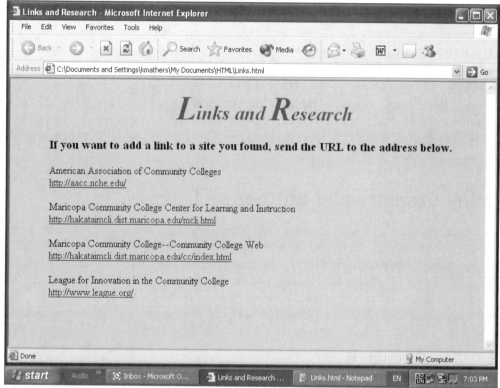

FIGURE 4.2 Page with links

Linking Within the Same Document

Linking to a different location in the same document is a lot like placing a bookmark in a word processing document. In both cases, you must identify and name the "destination", that is, the point in the document that the user is taken to when the link is clicked.

For example, if you want the user to go to a section that provides help, you place the following anchor tag at that location:

```
<A NAME="help">Help Section</A>
```

This tag names the section of the document "help", starting with the text "Help Section".

After naming a location in the document, you place the anchor tag around the text that you want the user to click. For example, if you want the user to click on the text, "For help on this topic", you would use the following anchor tag and Hypertext reference:

```
<A HREF="#help">For help on this topic</A>
```

When the user wants help, he can click on the text "For help on this topic" and he will be transferred to the Help Section of the document. Including a link back to the original location for the user is also common courtesy on the Web. To do this, give the original location a name, such as "top", and include the anchor tags to return the user to the top of the document.

Notice that when linking to another document, the Hypertext Reference in the opening <A> tag contains the complete URL of the document. When linking to another location in the same document, the Hypertext Reference in the opening <A> tag contains a # followed by the name of the anchor that you set.

Using Graphics and Buttons as Links

Buttons can be used to allow users to return to the home page, return to the top of the current page, get more information or be transferred to another page. You can create buttons using a graphics program such as PaintShop Pro, an excellent shareware program. You can also find numerous clipart buttons on the Web. To make a button a link, you use the anchor tag in the same way you used it in the previous section to create hypertext. That is, you place the anchor tags around the IMG tag. This syntax can also be used to for any image on your Web page. For example, a small, thumbnail image can be loaded quickly, and if you place anchor tags around the image, it can be used to link to the full-size graphic.

By placing the IMG tag within the anchor tags, the pointer will change to a hand when the user points to the image, indicating that the image is a link.

A button or icon can be used to link the user to another page. For example, The Hunger Site, which helps fight world hunger, has the user click a button to donate food. When you click the Donate Free Food button, you are connected to a page detailing which sponsors have paid for your donation. See Figure 4.3 below.

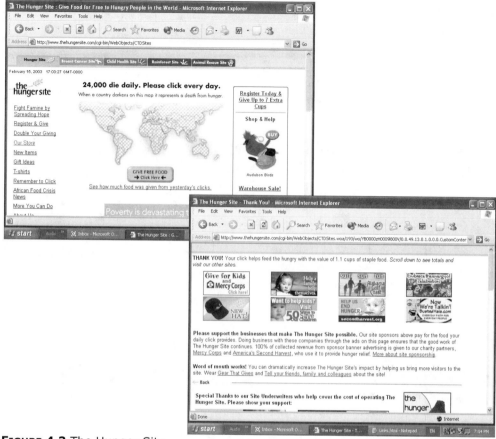

FIGURE 4.3 The Hunger Site

Creating an Email Link

You will want to make it easy for people who visit your Web site to get in touch with you. One simple way is to create an e-mail button. When the user clicks the button, a pre-addressed e-mail form displays.

This type of link is called a mail to link because the reserved word "mailto" will precede your email address in the Hypertext Reference.

The following code is used to display a mail button and text for the user to click.

```
<A HREF="mailto:sue@efn.com"> <IMG SRC="mail button.gif"> </A>
<A HREF="mailto:jim@telnet.org">Email Jim Smith</A>
```

Figure 4.4 shows the result of this code.

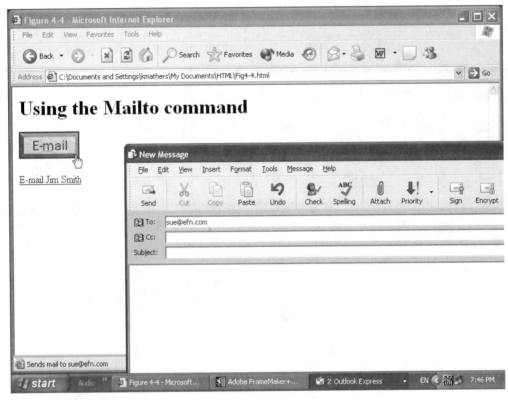

FIGURE 4.4 Mailto

Linking External Style Sheets

In addition to defining tag styles in the Head of the document, you can also create a separate document containing all your style definitions. Then, you simply link your HTML document to the style sheet, and all the formatting is still carried out by the Web browser.

There are a few reasons why it is preferable to use external style sheets:

♦   You can have many HTML documents share the same style sheet so that you do not have to repeat the same style definitions in each document. This makes for consistent formatting across all the pages of the Web site, no matter when the page was created.

♦   You can make changes to the style sheet without having to edit the HTML document. Again, if you have a multi-page Web site, using an external style sheet means that you only need to modify styles in one place. If you defined the styles in each HTML document, you would have to go through every single one in order to make any style changes across the entire site!

- Though we will not be covering how to do so in this book, it is also possible to have the Web browser selectively load style sheets, based on criteria like the media (computer screen, printed page, handheld device, aural (speech synthesis), etc.) Maintaining each set of style definitions in a separate document makes it easier to manage them.

The code used to link an external style sheet uses the LINK tag:

```
<LINK rel="stylesheet" type="text/css" href="web_styles.css">
```

You always place the link to an external style sheet in the HEAD of the HTML document. In the above example, the "rel" attribute set to "stylesheet" means that the page has only one stylesheet. The type of "text/css" means it is a text document containing the style definitions in Cascading Style Sheet (CSS) language—all the style defintions used in this book are written in CSS. This is the standard style language for HTML. The "href" attribute designates the URL for the file. In this example, the css file is located in the same location as the HTML document.

A css file is a simple text file, which you can easily create using Notepad. Figure 4.5 shows a sample external css file.

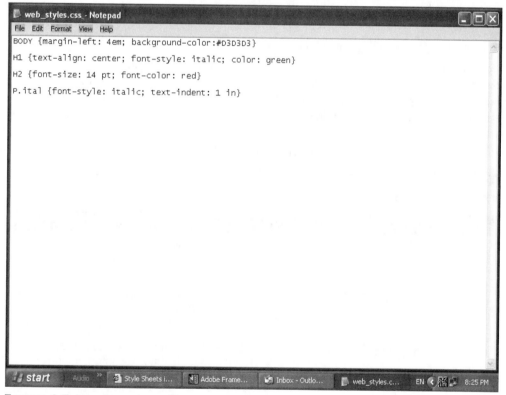

FIGURE 4.5 An external css file

Creating a Form

Forms provide the capacity to get input from site visitors by allowing them to enter information into blank areas and make selections from options. This type of interaction with visitors to your Web site is a powerful feature.

A form is created in the Web document between the opening and closing <BODY> tags, and the entire body of the form is contained between the opening and closing <FORM> tags. The ACTION attribute is mandatory because it specifies the URL where data from the form is to be sent. The action here is simply to mail to an e-mail address. The METHOD attribute has only two possible values: GET and POST. When you use GET, the default value, the data is added to the end of the URL and sent to the server as a variable. POST sends a separate stream of data to the server and is used to send the information on the form to an e-mail address.

When the visitor fills out a form, the information will be sent to the owner of the page at the e-mail address specified by the ACTION attribute. For example,

```
<FORM ACTION="mailto:lindae@uoregon.edu" METHOD=POST>
    contents of the form
</FORM>
```

There are no spaces allowed in the ACTION section of the FORM tag.

After setting up the opening and closing <FORM> tags in your document, you are ready to define the user-input fields (data elements) that will appear on the form. Form fields are the same as fields used in database software or in the address file for a mail merge. That is, they are the individual elements that make up the data for one person - for example, Last Name might be one field, and City another field.

You receive input from the user with the <INPUT> tag. You need to specify the type of input by the TYPE attribute. The most common type of input is TEXT.

TABLE 4.1 ATTRIBUTES

ATTRIBUTE	DESCRIPTION
SIZE	Defines the size of the text input box on your form, in number of characters. The default setting is 20 characters.
MAXLENGTH	Defines the number of characters that will be accepted (because the user can actually type more characters than the size of the box).
NAME	Gives the text input box a data element name that identifies the information.

This is the format for the <INPUT> tag:

```
<INPUT TYPE="TEXT">
```

This HTML tag places a text input box on the form. You can further define the text input with attributes. Table 4.1 lists the attributes.

The following example sets the size of the input box as 30 characters, with a maximum input of 40 characters from the user. The name of the box is "username":

```
Enter Your Name:
<INPUT TYPE="TEXT" SIZE="30" MAXLENGTH="40" NAME="username">
```

Figure 4.6 shows the result of this command.

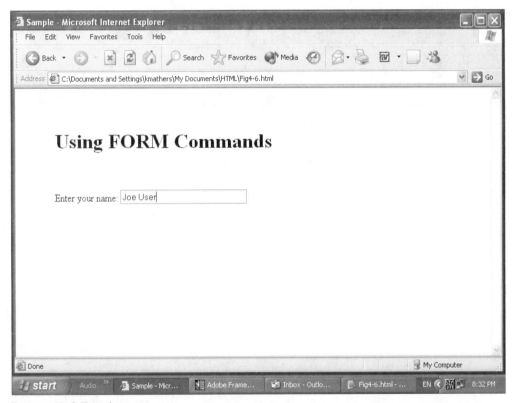

FIGURE 4.6 Text box

You can make your form easier to use by providing radio buttons for selecting one option from a group of options. You also can provide check boxes for selecting one or more options in a group.

To create radio buttons, specify the <INPUT> type as RADIO. You must provide a NAME attribute for the group of radio buttons—for example, using the word "Amount" as the name for a group of donation options.

After specifying the name of the group of buttons, you must specify the individual buttons contained within the group by using the VALUE option. Whereas the group name stays the same for the group of buttons, the value for each individual button is unique. The value is the information that gets passed on from the form to the e-mail (in this case), or to whatever else is handling the script.

The text following the closing angle bracket (>) appears on-screen after the button explaining the button choice to the user. For example,

```
<INPUT TYPE="RADIO" NAME="CITY" VALUE="Boston">Boston
<INPUT TYPE="RADIO" NAME="CITY" VALUE="Cambridge">Cambridge
```

With radio buttons, the user can choose only one of the radio button options in any set or group. Figure 4.7 shows the result of the code.

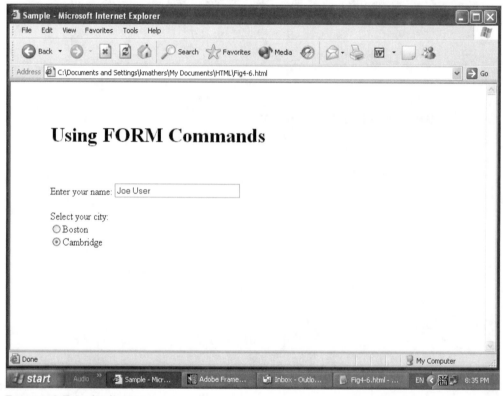

FIGURE 4.7 Radio buttons

The only difference between radio buttons and check boxes is that the user can make multiple selections in a set of check boxes. The procedure for creating check boxes is similar to the one for creating radio buttons. To create check boxes, you use the CHECKBOX attribute with the <INPUT>.

You can have a single check box for the user to select one option, or you can provide a group of check boxes. Check boxes are also grouped together using the same NAME attribute, and you define the value for the check box with the VALUE attribute.

An example of a single check box is:

```
<INPUT TYPE="CHECKBOX" VALUE="information"> Please send
information
```

An example of a set of grouped checkboxes is:

```
<INPUT TYPE="CHECKBOX" NAME="animal" VALUE="panda">Giant
Pandas<BR>
<INPUT TYPE="CHECKBOX" NAME="animal" VALUE="turtle">Sea
Turtles<BR>
<INPUT TYPE="CHECKBOX" NAME="animal" VALUE="crane">Sandhill
Cranes<BR>
<INPUT TYPE="CHECKBOX" NAME="animal" VALUE="tiger">Tigers<BR>
<INPUT TYPE="CHECKBOX" NAME="animal" VALUE="whale">Blue Whales
```

Figure 4.8 shows the result of the above code.

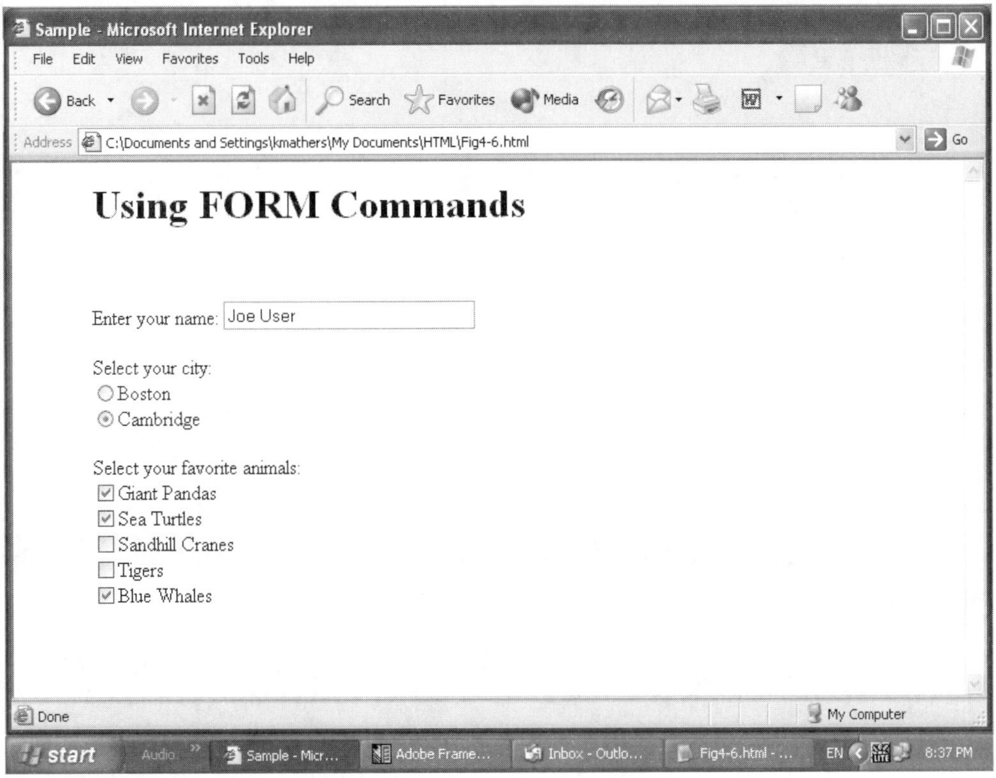

FIGURE 4.8 Check boxes

You can provide the user with several options by creating a list box and placing the options in the list. You use the opening and closing <SELECT> tags to enclose the list options. Each item on the list is then identified with the <OPTION> tag. In the following example, a list named County will be displayed, with the options Franklin, Lane, and Jefferson.

```
<SELECT NAME="County">
    <OPTION>Franklin
    <OPTION>Lane
    <OPTION>Jefferson
</SELECT>
```

Figure 4.9 shows the result of this code.

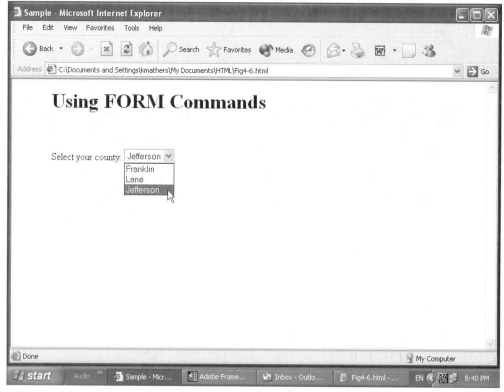

FIGURE 4.9 Drop-down list

If you want the user to be able to input a large amount of text, create a text area on the form with the <TEXTAREA> tag. As with other text fields, you can use the NAME attribute to define the <TEXTAREA> data, and you can also define the size of the area. The default size of the text area is 40 characters wide by 4 rows long.

To change the size from the default, use the COLS and ROWS attributes:

```
<TEXTAREA NAME="response" COLS="20" ROWS="10">
</TEXTAREA>
```

Figure 4.10 shows the result of this code.

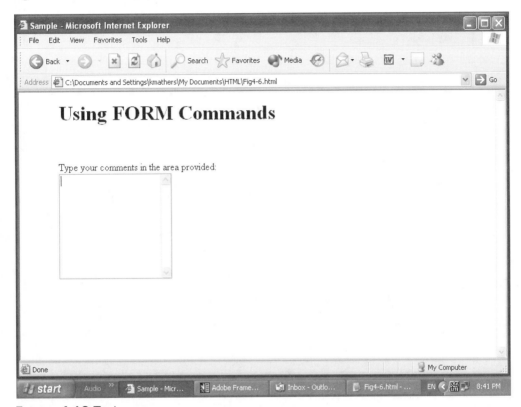

FIGURE 4.10 Text area

The standard way for a user to send form information to the server is to use a Submit button. When the user clicks the Submit button, the form contents are sent to the URL defined in the ACTION attribute of the opening <FORM) tag. The submit button's VALUE attribute allows you to define the text that appears on the button. If you do not include the VALUE attribute, the text Submit Query will appear on the button. This is the format:

```
<INPUT TYPE="SUBMIT" VALUE="Send Data">
```

When you include a Submit button on a form, you should also include a Reset button. The Reset button clears all fields and resets all the form's default settings.

You can also use the VALUE option to change the text on the Reset button. The default text is Reset. This command creates a Reset button with the text "Clear" on it:

```
<INPUT TYPE="RESET" VALUE="Clear">
```

Figure 4.11 show the result of this code.

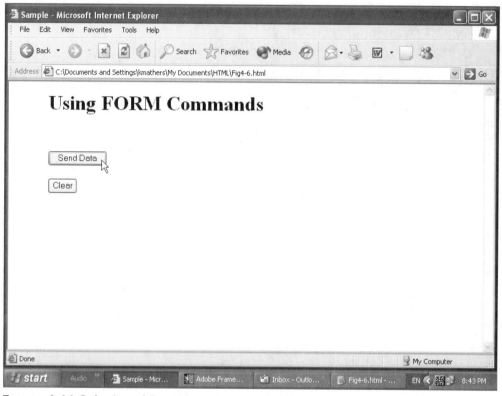

FIGURE 4.11 Submit and Reset buttons

❖ TRY THIS!

Link Your Documents to Others

Make your Web site interactive by including the following:

- ☑ Links to other documents
- ☑ Links to other locations on the World Wide Web
- ☑ Links within the document
- ☑ A link to an external style sheet
- ☑ Buttons that link to other documents
- ☑ An e-mail link to your e-mail address
- ☑ A form to receive information from your visitors

Enhancing and Evaluating a Home Page

- Using Frames
- Applying Navigation Rules
- Formatting Guidelines
- Using Graphics Effectively
- Evaluating the Overall Impact of the Web Page
- Publishing Your Web Page
- ❖ *Improve Your Web Page*

This chapter introduces some additional methods to add depth to your Web site. In this chapter, you will also learn how to objectively analyze your site's presentation, and how to publish it when completed.

Using Frames

Frames allow you to divide the screen display into sections. Each section then has a separate HTML file loaded into it.

You create the files loaded into the frames just as you would any HTML file. However, you must create a different type of HTML file to divide the screen and to load the files. Instead of containing a body section that uses the opening and closing <BODY> tags, you use the opening and closing <FRAMESET> tag to define the number and size of the frames. For example,

```
<FRAMESET cols="20%, 80%"> contents of frame
</FRAMESET>
```

This tag defines a screen divided into two vertical sections. The section on the left will take up 20% of the display, and the section on the right will take up 80% of the display.

To divide the screen into three horizontal bands, you would use the following:

```
<FRAMESET rows="30%, 40%, *"> contents of frame
</FRAMESET>
```

The asterisk * is used to tell the browser to use up the rest of the available display. It is also possible to define the number of pixels for each section; however, it is not recommended because of the difference in resolution from one display to another. Figure 5.1 shows a whimsical use of the frames command to construct faces randomly.

You can also combine horizontal and vertical frames so that you have both horizontal and vertical sections on the same display. However, keep your display simple—do not include too many frames. The result may be that the user only sees a small portion of several documents.

After you establish the number and size of the frames, you use the <FRAME> tag to set up the contents of each frame. The <FRAME> tag has several attributes, defined in Table 5.1.

FIGURE 5.1 Classic faces game

TABLE 5.1 <FRAME> ATTRIBUTES

ATTRIBUTE	RESULT
SRC="file.html" scrolling="yes/no/auto"	Places the file in the frame.If scrolling equals yes, then the frame will have a scrollbar. If scrolling equals no, then the frame will not have a scroll bar. If scrolling equals auto, and if the browser determines that a scrollbar is needed, then one will be included.
NAME="name"	Will give the frame the name contained in quotation marks.
NORESIZE	Will keep the user from being able to resize the frame.

In order to include information for users who do not have browsers capable of displaying frames, it is a common practice to use the opening and closing <NOFRAMES> tags to include information for the user. For example,

```
<NOFRAMES>This document can only be viewed by a browser capable of
displaying frames.</NOFRAMES>
```

The <NOFRAMES> tag is ignored by browsers that display frames.

You can allow the user to click in one frame and load the file in another frame, as this Faces2 game demonstrates in Figure 5.2.

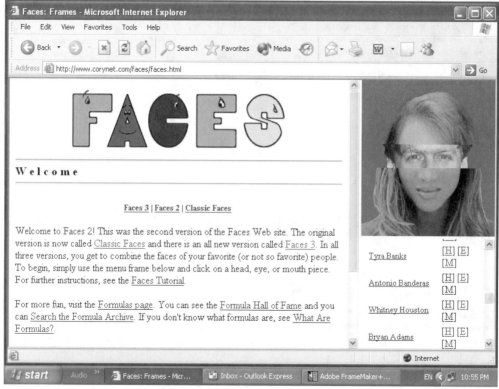

FIGURE 5.2 The Faces 2 game

For example, you can use the frame's feature to create a menu that will stay on the screen at all times. When the user clicks a menu choice in one frame, the file is loaded into another frame. For example, in Figure 5.3 the right frame displays the menu.

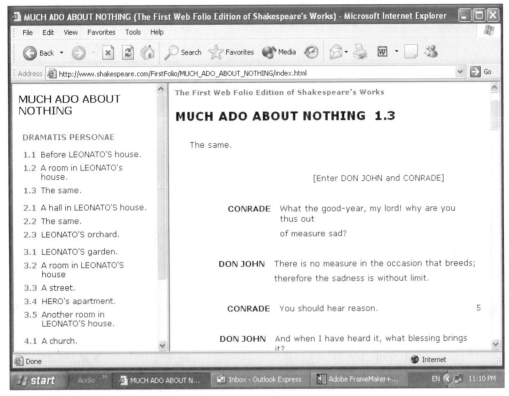

FIGURE 5.3 Shakespeare.com

In order to load the .html file in another frame, you need to include the TARGET attribute with the <A HREF> tag, making the target location the name of the frame defined in the <FRAME> tag.

```
<A HREF="ocean.html" TARGET="main">the ocean</A>
```

When the visitor clicks on the text, "the ocean", which is contained in the menu frame, the file ocean.html will load into the frame named "main".

Applying Navigation Rules

The main navigation rule for Web design is to let the user know where he is at all times and help him to proceed to the information he is looking for. Nothing is more frustrating than not being able to navigate in a Web site because the developer assumed everyone would visit his site starting from the top of the site.

Other tips for making your Web site easy to navigate:

+ Avoid useless clicking and page loads. Clicking through two or three extra levels that are not necessary will turn visitors away.

+ Use the top page to grab the user's attention and explain what the site contains. Using an attractive list of links to other sections of the document will help load the page faster and allow the visitor to see, at a glance, what you have to offer. This will entice visitors to load subsequent pages.

+ Place the most important information first because many visitors will not go past your first page.

+ If your site is large, think about including Next and Previous buttons on every page to direct visitors through the site. Especially useful is a Home link back to the first page of the Web site, so that no matter where a reader ends up, they can always get right back to the main page if necessary.

+ Place all your links in one location.

+ Do not place "under construction" signs on Web pages. Visitors get frustrated waiting for a page to load only to find out that there is nothing there.

+ Remember to do your planning first before you even start to code. Plan for the Web—do not just take a paper document and put it on a Web page with lots of bells and whistles. You should think about the way a user will navigate your site. Plan to present them with the information they are looking for.

+ Do not let information or links get out-of-date. The site must always be current.

+ Let the visitor know what is new so that a repeat visitor will have a reason to return to your site and to stay.

+ Give visitors reasons to bookmark your site by providing valuable information.

+ Include dates on the page to show updated information.

+ Always include a way back to the top of the presentation.

+ Never allow a page to be a dead end; that is, every page should have a link to the home page.

Formatting Guidelines

Have a consistent theme or include unifying elements throughout the entire site by using colors, bullets, buttons, and fonts that match or complement each other. Place the logo in the same place on every page so the visitor knows where he is. Check out the feel of site—a busy or black background with dungeon and dragon art probably does not lend itself to a business site. Format the site for the type of information you are including and remember your audience.

Remember that simple is the best. Simple pages load fast, and users can see at a glance if the site is relevant to them. Text can be divided with lines, formatted with lists that include links to more detailed information. Choice of font and text size is extremely important, as well. Too many frames, too much animation, blinking text, text of too many sizes and colors, and large images all reduce the appeal of the page. Even too much text will turn away visitors. . Fonts and styles are central to a site's readability.

Using Graphics Effectively

Remember that not all graphics on the Web are free; many are the work of artists who copyright those images and make their living from their art. Always read the copyright notice at any graphics site and adhere to the request of the site owner. If an image belongs to someone else and you want to use it on your web site, be prepared to negotiate for permission.

Remember that you can scan logos, photographs, or your own art to include on your site.

One tip is to use the same graphic, such as the company logo, on every page because most browsers store images in a cache. This will enable the browser to load the graphic file from the cache rather than having to download it, speeding up your pages.

Remember to include images only if they are relevant to the content and are an important part of the page design.

Evaluating the Overall Impact of the Web Page

Have you included too many busy graphics, as shown in Figure 5.4?

Have you included too much unformatted text, such as the page shown in Figure 5.5?

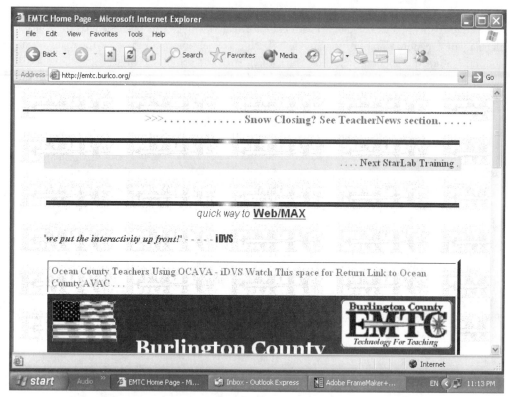

FIGURE 5.4 A page with too many flashy graphics

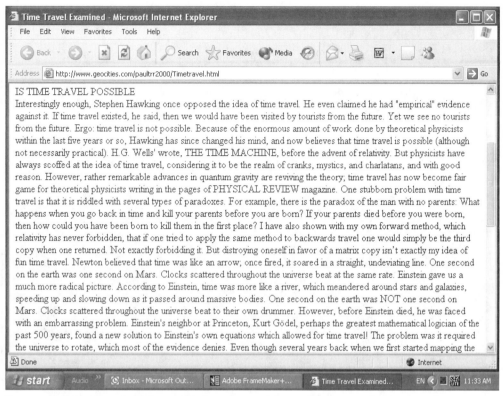

FIGURE 5.5 Too much unformatted text

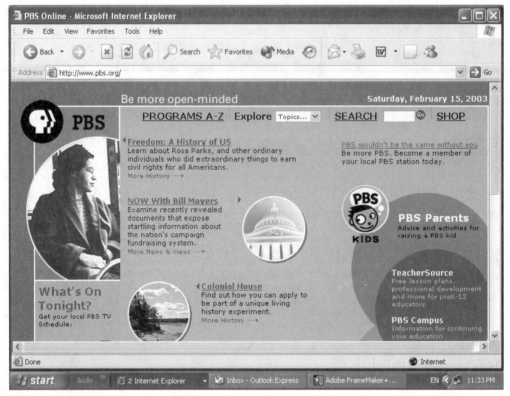

FIGURE 5.6 PBS

Does the top page invite visitors in and grab their attention by clearly showing them what you have to offer? Figure 5.6 shows a top page that has impact.

Give your URL to others and get feedback from friends and colleagues. Take their advice and spend time making your Web site user-friendly.

Publishing Your Web Page

After your web document is easy to navigate, fast to load, free of grammar and spelling errors, all content is accurate, and you have checked it out in several browsers, you are ready to publish it. Some people think that others can access their document because it is on their computer's hard drive and they are linked to the World Wide Web. This is not the case; you have to place your Web documents along with any graphic files on a Web server. If you have an Internet Service Provider, you should check to see what kind of services they offer. Do they impose any types of limits? Do they support all the features that you want? What do they charge? If you are designing a commercial site, you might explore maintaining your own Web server so that you have more control over security and management of the site.

You can also search the Web for services that host Web sites to find the one that best suits your needs.

In order to transfer your Web page from your computer to your Web host, you will need to use FTP—File Transfer Protocol. Two common shareware FTP software packages are CUTE FTP and WS-FTP. Both are easy to find and simple to use. Your Web host will supply you with the necessary information to connect and upload your Web site, such as the Hostname, URL, and Login name.

After you publish your site, you need to help people find it. The first step is to register your site with the major search engines. However, before doing this, you should include META tags in the <HEAD> section of the top page. This can help ensure that your page is indexed and described properly. You use the <META> tag to list keywords found in the document and to create a description of the Web site. When search engines (which use spiders or robots) index your site, they will fill their database with the text and description you placed in the <META> tag.

To create a description of your site, use the "description" attribute, and to create a list of keywords, use the "keywords" attribute, and then list the keywords separated by commas. Here is an example of the <META> tag for a technical writer's site:

```
<HEAD>
<TITLE>Cyber-Writer.com</TITLE>

<META name="description" content="Author of computer text books,
online help systems, Web pages, and other technical documents">

<META name="keywords" content="computer books, technical writing,
textbooks, online help, editing, technical editing, Web
development">

</HEAD>
```

After you have included the <META> tags, you are ready to register your site with the search engines. Some of the major search engines are: Yahoo! AltaVista, Lycos, Excite, Infoseek, and Web Crawler.

Make sure to use the URL of your site on your business cards, stationery, and other business documents.

After you have published your Web presentation, keep it maintained and up-to-date. Periodically check all links to make sure that they are still active, and add new updated information to your page so that you will have repeat visitors.

❖ TRY THIS!

Improve Your Web Page

Make improvements to your Web page by:

- ☑ Including <META> tags in the <HEAD> section
- ☑ Testing your site on friends
- ☑ Checking for all spelling and grammar errors
- ☑ Researching Web hosts
- ☑ Learning about FTP software

Adding JavaScript to a Web Page

- Getting Started with JavaScript
- Hiding JavaScript from Older Browsers
- Becoming Familiar with JavaScript
- Writing Simple Scripts
- Creating Functions

❖ *Add JavaScript to Your Web Page*

This chapter provides a basic introduction to the JavaScript scripting language, and provides instruction on how to insert some simple JavaScript scripts into a Web page.

Getting Started with JavaScript

JavaScript is a programming or scripting language that Web designers use to build sites that will respond to specific user actions.

Some examples of JavaScript scripts include: displaying messages to the user that appear on the Web page, in an alert box, or in the status line; displaying browser information, including the type of browser and plug-ins available; validating form information; creating animation; creating clocks and calendars; and, in general, performing actions in response to the user.

Scripting languages allow you to write programs by defining the list of actions that should occur. They require only a basic knowledge of programming concepts, which makes a scripting language much easier for non-programmers to learn.

Sometimes people confuse JavaScript with the programming language Java. JavaScript is a simple scripting language designed to work with your browser. The script you write is placed right in the Web document, and the JavaScript code is interpreted by a browser. Java is a more complex language and requires a compiler to translate the program.

Netscape Communications Corporation developed JavaScript for use on Web pages, so JavaScript programs are most often run from within browser software. However, unlike HTML, JavaScript programs can encounter compatibility problems between browsers. Most problems can be avoided by using basic JavaScript features that have cross-platform support, by hiding JavaScript scripts from older browsers (as you will see later in this section), or by writing a script that detects which browser the user is running and then displays Web pages based on that information.

Since JavaScript programs can be typed right into your HTML document, you can use the tools with which you are already familiar. There are several different ways to embed JavaScript into your HTML document, each with different advantages:

*   JavaScript embedded between <SCRIPT> and </SCRIPT> tags.

JavaScript scripts placed between SCRIPT tags are executed after the page loads. They can be placed in the Body of the document, but most often it is best to place a JavaScript in the Head element of the page. The Head of the HTML document is always loaded before the Body.

Because HTML is evaluated as it is loaded, if an event handler attempts to run a piece of JavaScript that has not yet been loaded, it will not work. To get around this, JavaScript is most often placed in the document Head so that it is completely loaded before events in the Body of the document try to use it.

When typing a JavaScript program into the <HEAD> or <BODY> sections of the HTML document, you must place the entire script within the opening and closing <SCRIPT> tags.

```
<HTML>
<HEAD> <TITLE>page title</TITLE>
<SCRIPT>
    a JavaScript script in the HEAD section is typed here
```

```
</SCRIPT>
<BODY>
   <H1>page heading</H1>
   <SCRIPT>
      a JavaScript script in the BODY section is typed here
   </SCRIPT>
</BODY>
</HTML>
```

The <SCRIPT> tag includes optional attributes including the TYPE attribute and the SRC attribute. You should always use the TYPE attribute with the <SCRIPT> tag because it tells the browser displaying the Web page which scripting language was used to create the program. As more scripting languages are developed, browsers will need to be informed of the language used. For example, you would type the following:

```
<SCRIPT TYPE="text/javascript"> a JavaScript script is typed here
</SCRIPT>
```

♦ JavaScript can be stored externally from the HTML document. The library must have a .js extension, and the document must reside on a server.

A second optional attribute, SRC, is used to access an external JavaScript library file by specifying its URL. For example, for a file named library.js located at mysite.com, you would type the following:

```
<SCRIPT TYPE="text/javascript"
SRC="http://www.mysite.com/library.js">
</SCRIPT>
```

♦ JavaScript can be placed inside an HTML tag to respond to actions performed by the user (called an event handler), such as when the user points the mouse over a link. (See Event Handlers on page 79 for more details on event handlers.)

♦ JavaScript can also be placed in the body of a URL that uses the special javascript:// protocol. For example:

```
<A HREF="javascript:alert('Hello World')">Hello World</A>
```

Hiding JavaScript from Older Browsers

When older browsers encounter the <SCRIPT> tag, errors can result because they try to display the codes as HTML. One method used by programmers to keep older browsers from displaying error messages is to hide the actual script by placing the entire JavaScript script inside an HTML Comment tag. Remember that the HTML opening Comment tag <!-- and the closing Comment tag --> enclose text that will be ignored by the browser. In this case, browsers that can not display the JavaScript program will ignore it instead of trying to display it as regular HTML.

For example, you would type the following:

```
<SCRIPT TYPE="text/javascript">
    <!-- HIDE THE SCRIPT FROM OLDER BROWSERS
    the JavaScript script is typed here
    // END OF THE COMMENT -->
</SCRIPT>
```

Notice the two forward slashes (//) in the example that appear on the line that contains the text END OF THE COMMENT. To place a comment within a JavaScript script, you must start the line with two forward slashes (//). It is a good idea to place comments in your JavaScript scripts so that you will be able to remember what the script is supposed to do or to allow others to understand your script.

You can also use the <NOSCRIPT> tag that allows you to place alternative text on the screen for browsers that can not run the script. For example, text you place between the opening and closing <NOSCRIPT> tags will be displayed on the Web page. However, the <NOSCRIPT> tag is ignored if the script can be run. For example, you would type the following:

```
<SCRIPT TYPE="text/javascript">
    <!-- HIDE THE SCRIPT FROM OLDER BROWSERS
    the JavaScript script is typed here
    // END OF THE COMMENT -->
</SCRIPT>
<NOSCRIPT>
    Your browser can't display the results of the JavaScript
    <BR>
    Download a newer Web browser.
</NOSCRIPT>
```

Becoming Familiar with JavaScript

JavaScript is a simple example of object-oriented programming languages. In object-oriented programming, information is organized by objects that have certain characteristics and can be acted upon. JavaScript includes many built-in objects, and you can also create your own. For example, a Window is a built-in JavaScript object. An object has properties that describe it. A Window object includes a document property that identifies the HTML document that will be displayed in the window. It also includes a status property that defines the text which will appear in the status bar. The syntax for writing an object with its property is designated from left to right, that is, starting with the object first and separating it from the property with a period (object.property). For instance, to access the status bar of a window, you would type the following:

```
window.status
```

An object also has methods that describe what the object can do. For example, a Window object can open other windows; it can come into focus, meaning that a window behind another window moves to the front, or it can be blurred, meaning that a window is moved out of focus or behind other windows. The syntax for writing an object with its method is designated from left to right, that is, starting with the object first and separating it from the method with a period (object.method()). For instance, to open a window, you would type the following:

```
window.open()
```

Two parentheses must always be typed immediately following the method. If no further information is needed, the parentheses will remain empty.

JavaScript object properties can also be objects themselves. For example, the Window object discussed previously included the document property that is the actual HTML document displayed in the window. The document property is also an object that has properties. In order for this system to work so that it is easier to identify objects, properties and methods, JavaScript makes use of a hierarchy of objects called the Document Object Model, or DOM. This hierarchy starts with the largest built-in object and works down. For example, if a window contains a document that contains a form with text, a submit button, radio buttons, and check boxes, the hierarchy would look like the following diagram:

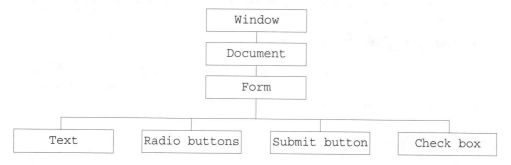

This diagram is only a small portion of the DOM. For more information on the JavaScript Document Object Model, visit the Netscape site at http://www.netscape.com.

Another aspect of JavaScript programs is events, which are actions performed by the user that trigger other actions. For example, the user might point to a graphic, type text in a form, or click on a button. You can write scripts that detect when an event happens and then respond to the event; these are called event handlers. Event handlers are placed inside HTML tags like attributes. The syntax is typed as follows:

```
<HTML tag with attributes
eventHandler="action">
```

For example, you will use the following event handler in the next section.

```
<INPUT type="button" value="Open the Page"
onClick="window.open('http://www.goducks.com')">
```

Event handlers follow a standard syntax: the first word, such as "on", is always in lowercase; each word in the event name is capitalized, such as on "Click"; and the entire event handler contains no spaces. Table 6.1 lists several useful event handlers and their associated objects.

TABLE 6.1 EVENT HANDLERS

EVENT HANDLER	OBJECTS	DESCRIPTION
onClick	Button, checkbox, radio button, hypertext link,submit button, reset button	The user clicks on one of the objects.
onLoad	Document, graphic, window	A page or image is loaded into the browser.
onMouseOver	Hyperlink, image map	The user moves the mouse over an object (like a hypertext link).
onMouseOut	Hyperlink, image map	The user moves the mouse off the object.

Writing Simple Scripts

A simple JavaScript program that you can include on your Web page opens an alert box and places the text you designate in the dialog box. You might use an alert box to feature sale items on a commercial site, as shown in Figure 6.1.

FIGURE 6.1 An alert box

You could call the alert box by typing the following code in the body of the document:

```
<SCRIPT LANGUAGE="JavaScript">
    <!-- Hide from old browsers
    //places an alert box on the screen
        window.alert("50% off selected items!");
    //end of the comment -->
</SCRIPT>
```

However, because Window is the default top-level object, you do not need to type it in the script. You can simply type the line as follows:

```
alert("50% off selected items!");
```

Notice two important syntax elements of this script:

1. The text that appears in the alert box is placed within quotation marks inside the parentheses.
2. The JavaScript statement ends with a semicolon. The semi-colon is used as the end punctuation for all JavaScript statements.

The hierarchy for this script is that the default top-level object window uses the method "alert" with a prompt.

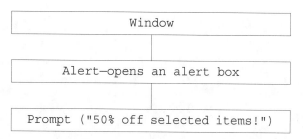

You can create a second script that also places text on a Web page by using the command document.write ("text that will appear in the document"). Whatever appears inside the parentheses will be written to the document. The following script gets the date that the document was last modified from the server and writes it on the Web page, as shown in Figure 6.2.

You would type the following in the BODY:

```
<P>This page was last modified:
<SCRIPT TYPE="text/javascript">
    <!-- Hide from old browsers
    //writes the date the document was saved
    document.write(document.lastModified);
    //end of the comment -->
</SCRIPT>
```

The hierarchy for this script starts with the top-level object document and its method "write". The method's parentheses contain the object document and its property "lastModified". The actual program gets the date the document was saved and writes it to the document after the text *This page was last modified.*

This page was last modified:

02/16/2003 21:44:54

FIGURE 6.2 The date appears on the Web page

A third simple script that you can write opens a second Web document in a new window when the user clicks a button, as shown in Figures 6.3 and 6.4.

Oregon Ducks

FIGURE 6.3 The button the user clicks to display the new window

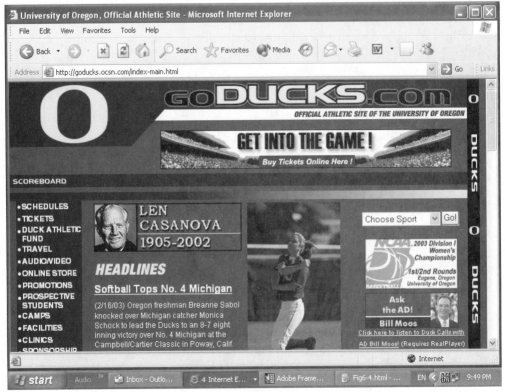

FIGURE 6.4 The new window displays with the document

This script is an example of an event handler; that is, the JavaScript appears inside an HTML tag. To place the button on the Web page, use the <FORM> tags as follows:

```
<FORM>
    <INPUT type="button" value="Oregon Ducks"
    onClick="window.open('http://www.goducks.com')">
</FORM>
```

The HTML code used by this script (FORM INPUT type equals "button") creates a button that contains the text Oregon Ducks. The JavaScript onClick event handler opens the new window when the user clicks the button. The document designated by the URL is placed in the new window.

A fourth script could be used to place text in the status bar when the user points to linked text. For example, if you want to tell the user to bookmark your page before leaving to go to the GoDucks.com site, you would include the following script that makes use of the OnMouseOver and OnMouseOut events:

```
<A HREF="http://www.goducks.com"
onMouseOver="window.status='Please bookmark this site before you
leave!';return true"
onMouseOut="window.status='';return true">Oregon Ducks</A>
```

Notice that the onMouseOut contains an empty opening and closing single quotation mark to remove the text from the status bar when the user moves the mouse off the link. Also notice the text *return true* that is used with the two event handlers. It is necessary to display the text in the status bar more than once. The result of this code is shown in Figure 6.5.

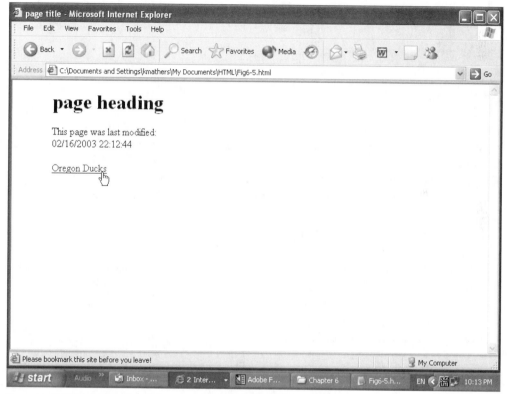

FIGURE 6.5 The result of the window.status code

Creating Functions

The scripts we have created so far are simple lists of instructions that would occur once on the Web page. To extend your programming abilities, you can create JavaScript functions that group statements together for a particular purpose, and they can be used more than once on the page. Creating a function is a two-step process:

1. Define a function in the <HEAD> section.

2. Call the function from within the <BODY> of the document.

To define a function, you would use the following syntax:

```
<HEAD>
   <SCRIPT TYPE="text/javascript">
      <!-- hide from old browsers
      //comment that describes the function
      function name (parameter 1, parameter 2)
      {
          JavaScript statements
      }
      //end of comment -->
   </SCRIPT>
</HEAD>
```

The previous example hides the JavaScript from old browsers and then places the word function in the script to declare that you are creating a function. The name of the function follows. You should name functions something meaningful, start the name with a character, and do not include any spaces in the name. If necessary, parameters, such as variables, can appear in the parentheses. The left-pointing brace ({) marks the beginning of the JavaScript statements that the function will perform. The right-pointing brace (}) marks the end of the JavaScript statements and the end of the function.

To call the function once it is defined, you use the function's name in a <SCRIPT> tag or as an event handler as part of an HTML tag.

Suppose that you want your Web document to be responsive to users by allowing them to change the background color when they click on certain buttons. Your script would need to place buttons on the screen that would change the color scheme when clicked. Because each button would contain much of the same scripting, this example is a perfect candidate for a function because you can write the code once and call it several times.

You would create the JavaScript as follows:

```html
<HTML>
<HEAD><TITLE>JavaScript Test</TITLE>
    <SCRIPT TYPE="text/javascript">
        <!-- hide from old browsers
        //the colorscheme function changes the background color
        function colorscheme(bg)
        {
            document.bgColor=bg;
        }
        //End of Comment -->
    </SCRIPT>
</HEAD>

<BODY>
<H1 style="text-align: center">Test of Color Scheme Function</H1>
<P>Click a button to change the background color of the page.</P>

<FORM>
    <INPUT type="button" value="Yellow"
    onClick="colorscheme('#FFFF00')">

    <INPUT type="button" value="Green"
    onClick="colorscheme('#00FF00')">

    <INPUT type="button" value="Magenta"
    onClick="colorscheme('#FF00FF')">
</FORM>

</BODY>
</HTML>
```

The results can be seen in Figures 6.6 and 6.7.

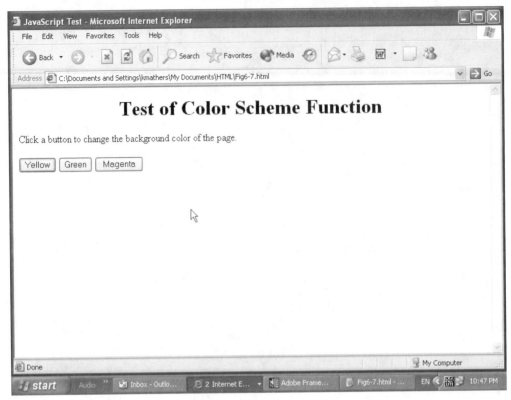

FIGURE 6.6 The page with the buttons

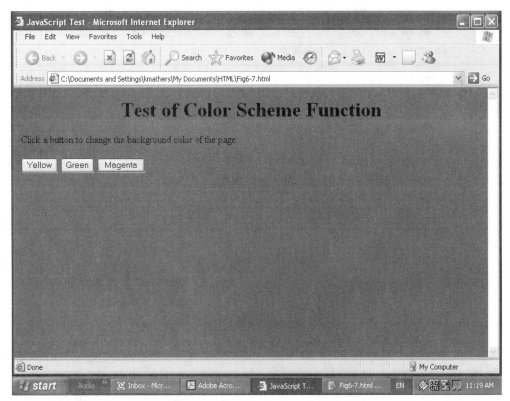

FIGURE 6.7 The page after the magenta button is clicked

Notice that the function makes use of a variable, which can be used to hold numbers or text. In this case the *bg* variable will be the color designated by the hexadecimal number that is passed to the function when the button is clicked.

❖ TRY THIS!

Add JavaScript to Your Web Page

☑ Using the design you created in the previous chapters, include a JavaScript alert box with text.

☑ Include a JavaScript script that places text on the screen.

☑ Include a JavaScript script that opens a new window that contains a document.

☑ Include a JavaScript script that places text in the status bar.

☑ Include a JavaScript script that calls a function when the mouse is clicked on an object.

Appendix A: URL Resources

This chapter lists over 250 Web sites which you can consult for useful information about Web design, or which you can explore for their design features. Use your browser's View>Source menu command to study the HTML syntax that produces the page. You can copy and modify the code and use it in your own projects.

Arts

Galleries and museums, paintings and photography are showcased by these sites.

3D Artists
www.raph.com/3dartists

American Photography
www.pbs.org/ktca/americanphotography

Art.com
www.art.com

Artcyclopedia
www.artcyclopedia.com

Artmuseum.net
www.artmuseum.net

ArtDaily
www.artdaily.com

Art Vision International
www.aabc.com

BestArt.com
www.bestart.com

The Metropolitan Museum of Art
www.metmuseum.org

National Gallery of Art
http://www.nga.gov

Online Photography
www.onlinephotography.com

The Gallery Online
www.galleryonline.com

Auctions

These sites list countless items that can be bought or sold. If it has a value, you can find it on one of these sites.

Auction.com
www.auction.com

Auction Hunter
www.auctionhunter.com

Bargain.com
www.bargain.com/Auctions

BidOutlet
www.bidoutlet.com

Bidz.com
noreserve.bidz.com

Collector Online
www.collectoronline.com

eBay
www.ebay.com

Global Auction
global-auction.com

iCollector - Online Live Actions
www2.icollector.com

Internet Auction List
www.internetauctionlist.com

OnSale.com
www.onsale.com

UBid.com
www.ubid.com

Vintage Posters
www.onlineposterauction.com

Best of the Web - Reviews

These sites evaluate and rate other sites. Some award prizes in the form of graphics that can be displayed on winning sites. Well-rated sites and products are listed here.

Best of the Web
botw.org/links.html

Diamond Web Awards.com
www.diamondwebawards.com

The Web100
www.web100.com

Worldwide Village
www.worldvillage.com/sitereviews/
family.html

ZDNet Reviews
www.zdnet.com/reviews

Cool Sites

These sites have interesting designs, content, or multimedia.

CourseVector
www.coursevector.com

Discovery.com
www.discovery.com

Frontier Cybercenter
www.frontieronline.com/cybercenter/
tour/flash_content/index.html

Madonna
www.madonna.com/madonna

Media Design Interactive
www.mediadesigns.com

Netcams
www.channel4000.com/sh/
entertainment/netcams

Nasa
www.nasa.gov/multimedia/

National Geographic Online
www.nationalgeographic.com

National Geographic Magazine
www.nationalgeographic.com/ngm

Smithsonian Institution
smithsonian.org

Smithsonian National Zoo
natzoo.si.edu

World Wildlife Fund
www.worldwildlife.org

Careers/Jobs

These sites include job search tools as well as career advice.

AfterCollege for Jobseekers
www.thejobresource.com/jobseekers

Best Jobs USA
www.bestjobsusa.com

Career.com
www.career.com/

CareerBuilder.com
www.careerbuilder.com

Computer Jobs
www.computerwork.com

Employment Guide
www.employmentguide.com

Hospitality Jobs
www.hcareers.com

Monster
www.monster.com

Hot Jobs
hotjobs.yahoo.com

Software jobs
www.softwarejobs.com

TechEmployment.com
www.techemployment.com/home.html

TrueCareers
www.careercity.com

UsJobNet.com
usjobnet.com

Computer - Programming

These sites provide information about programming using a variety of languages.

Cprogramming.com
www.cprogramming.com

CGI101.com
www.cgi101.com

The CGI Resource Index
www.cgi-resources.com/Documentation/
CGI_Tutorials/

The Code Project
www.codeproject.com

Developer.com
www.developer.com

Cool Companies

These companies have fun, interesting sites which make users want to explore further, whether or not they want to buy the product.

Coca-Cola
www.cocacola.com

Disney Online
disney.go.com/park

Fila
www.fila.com

FUBU
www.fubu.com

Gatorade
www.gatorade.com

Kelloggs
www.kelloggs.com

Lego
www.lego.com

Levis
www.us.levi.com/spr03a/levi/home/
l_home.jsp

Nike
www.nike.com

Pepsi
www.pepsiworld.com

Entertainment

These sites list a variety of television, music, and movie sites.

ABC
abc.abcnews.go.com

Cirque du Soleil
www.cirquedusoleil.com

HBO
www.hbo.com

Live365.com
www.live365.com/index.live

MTV
www.mtv.com

NBC
www.nbc.com

PBS Online
www.pbs.org

Sundance Channel
www.sundancechannel.com

Warner Bros. Online
www2.warnerbros.com

Fitness

These sites provide general information on staying fit and healthy.

BodyTrends.com
www.bodytrends.com

CyberDiet
www.cyberdiet.com

Fitness Online
www.fitnessonline.com

Fitness Zone
www.fitnesszone.com

Health Finder
www.healthfinder.gov

HealthFitness.com
www.healthfitnesstips.com

Health World Online
www.healthy.net

Nutrition Online
www.nutritiononline.com

Runner's World
www.runnersworld.com

Roadrunner Sports
www.roadrunnersports.com

Shape.com
www.shape.com

Shape Up America
www.shapeup.org

Games

These sites include puzzles and downloadable multimedia games.

A2zArcade
www.a2zarcade.com

BaliHighway.com
www.balihighway.com

Bethesda Softworks
www.bethsoft.com

Brain Bashers
www.brainbashers.com

Games Domain
www.gamesdomain.com/indexus.html

Games.com
play.games.com/playgames

GarageGames
garagegames.com

The Official Microsoft Games Website
www.microsoft.com/games

Puzzle Express
www.puzzlexpress.com

Puzzle Depot
www.puzzledepot.com

WorldVillage Games
www.worldvillage.com/wvgames

Yahoo! Games
play.yahoo.com

Zone.com
www.zone.com

Government

Although most government agencies have their own website, only a few are listed here.

AirForce Link
www.af.mil

Central Intelligence Agency
www.cia.gov

FBI - Most Wanted
www.fbi.gov/mostwant/topten/
fugitives/fugitives.htm

FedWorld
www.fedworld.gov

FedStats
www.fedstats.gov

The Library of Congress
www.loc.gov/

National Institues of Health (NIH)
www.hih.gov

The Smoking Gun
www.thesmokinggun.com

United States Postal Service
www.usps.com

US Senate
www.senate.gov

US Supreme Court Multimedia Database
oyez.nwu.edu/

Supreme Court of the United States
www.supremecourtus.gov

Graphics

These sites include software sites and tips for graphic design.

3D Cafe
www.3dcafe.com

Adobe
www.adobe.com

Amabilis
www.amabilis.com

CADalog.com
www.cadalog.com

CGI Insider
www.cginsider.com/#

Corel Corporation
www3.corel.com

Jasc Software
www.jasc.com

LigthWave 3D
www.lightwave3d.com

PhotoShop Tips
www.adobe.com/products/tips/
photoshop.html

Rhinoceros
www.rhino3d.com

HTML

These sites provide tips and tutorials for beginners and advanced HTML users.

A Complete Guide to HTML
www.draac.com/html.html

Dave's HTML Guide
www.davesite.com/webstation/html/

HTML Clinic
www.htmlclinic

HTML Goodies
www.htmlgoodies.com

HTML Tutorials in Web Page Design
www.alternetwebdesign.com/
htmltutorial/index.htm

HTML Tutorial - Lesson Plan
www.alternetwebdesign.com/
htmltutorial/index.html

HTML With Style
www.webreference.com/html

Learning HTML for Kids of All Ages
www.goodellgroup.com/tutorial/
index.html

PageTutor.com
www.pagetutor.com

Internet Directories & Providers

These sites provides lists of other Internet sites and service providers.

AnyWho Internet Directory
www.anywho.com

Daily Overlook
www.thedaily.com/overlook.html

Directory of ISPs
thedirectory.org/index.sht

Essential Links
www.el.com

Galaxy Search Engine
www.einet.net

InfoSpace
www.infospace.com

ISP Finder
www.cleansurf.com/

Librarians' Index to the Internet
lii.org

The List: ISPs
thelist.internet.com

LookSmart
www.looksmart.com

Superpages.com SuperTopics
www.superpages.com/supertopics

WhatIs
whatis.techtarget.com
new.jsp

Java

These sites provide tips and tutorials for beginners and experts alike.

Developer's Daily Java
www.devdaily.com/java/

DeveloperWorks Java technology
www-106.ibm.com/developerworks/java

Free Java Help - Tutorials
www.freejavahelp.com/tutorial/
index.html

Gamelan.com - A Developer.com Site
http://www.developer.com/java/

Java Guru Self-Paced Course List
www.jguru.com/learn/index.jsp

JavaWorld
www.javaworld.com

The Java Tutorial
java.sun.com/docs/books/tutorial/
index.html

Kidstuff

These cool sites contain hours of fun and learning for kids of all ages.

4Kids Treehouse
www.4kids.com/4kidshome.html

A to Z Kids Stuff
www.atozkidsstuff.com/index.html

A&E Classroom
www.aetv.com/class/#

Crayola
www.crayola.com

Enchanted Learning Software
www.enchangedlearning.com/home.html

Fact Monster Online Almanac
www.factmonster.com

Kids' Castle
www.kidscastle.si.edu

Kids Space
www.kids-space.org

MSN Kidz
kids.msn.com/kidz

PBS Kids
pbskids.org

Scholastic.com
www.scholastic.com

Sesame Workshop
www.sesamestreet.com

Seussville
www.seussville.com/seussville

Yahooligans.com
www.yahooligans.com

More Cool Stuff

These sites have the answers to unusual questions, trivia, and interesting or unusual facts.

Braincandy Trivia
www.corsinet.com/trivia

CoolQuiz
www.coolquiz.com/trivia

eHow.com
www.ehow.com/home

HowStuffWorks
www.howstuffworks.com

SquirrelNet.com
www.squirrelnet.com

Useless Information
home.nycap.rr.com/useless/index.html

News and Information

These sites provide up-to-date information on current events, finanace, and sports.

ABC News
abcnews.go.com

CNN
www.cnn.com

CNN Money
money.cnn.com

ESPN.com
msn.espn.go.com/main.html

Fox News
www.foxnews.com

Info Junkie
www.infojunkie.com

MSNBC News
www.msnbc.com

NewsLink
newslink.org

Newseum
www.newseum.org

SportingNews.com
www.sportingnews.com

USAToday
www.usatoday.com

Yahoo! News Image Gallery
story.news.yahoo.com

Reference and Research

From academic research to current events and other facts, these sites bring a world of information to your desktop.

About.com
www.about.com

Academic Info
www.academicinfo.net/reffind.html

Bartleby.com - Great Books Online
www.bartleby.com

CIA Factbook
www.odci.gov/cia/publications/
factbook

Encyclopaedia Britannica
www.britannica.com

Exploratorium
www.exploratorium.edu

Internet Archive
www.archive.org

MSN Learning & Research - Reference
encarta.msn.com/encnet/features/
reference.aspx

Online Dictionary Net
www.online-dictionary.net

Refdesk Reference
www.refdesk.com

Webopedia
webopedia.internet.com

WebReference
www.webreference.com

The WWW Virtual Library
vlib.org

Search Engines

Use these sites to search for information, products, and answers to commonly asked questions.

AOL Search
search.aol.com

AltaVista
www.altavista.com

Ask Jeeves
www.ask.com/

Dogpile
www.dogpile.com/index.gsp

Google
groups.google.com

HotBot
www.hotbot.com

Lycos
www.lycos.com

MetaCrawler
www.metacrawler.com/index.html

Search.com
www.search.com

WebCrawler
www.webcrawler.com

Yahoo
www.yahoo.com

Security on the Web

These sites provide information and research about privacy issues on the Internet.

Counterpane Internet Security
www.counterpane.com

Electronic Privacy Information Center
epic.org

Firewalls and Security
www.digitex.cc/Products/
firewalls.html

Interhack Research
www.interhack.net

Internet Privacy Coalition
www.crypto.org

Internet Scambusters
www.scambusters.org

Junkbusters
www.junkbusters.com

SonicWALL
www.sonicwall.com

TRUSTe
www.etrust.com

Shopping - Books

These include new, used, and rare books, as well as audio and ebooks.

Abebooks.com
www.abebooks.com

Amazon.com
www.amazon.com

Audio Books
www.audible.com

Barnes & Noble
www.barnesandnoble.com

BookSense.com
www.booksense.com

BooksaMillion.com
http://www.booksamillion.com

Books on Tape
www.booksontape.com

eBooks.com
www.ebooks.com

eCampus.com
www.ecampus.com

VarsityBooks.com
www.varsitybooks.com

Shopping - General

These sites offer a variety of products and shopping related products.

Buy.com
www.buy.com

CDNow
www.cdnow.com

BestBuy
www.bestbuy.com

Bluefly.com
www.bluefly.com

DealTime
www1.dealtime.com

Gap Online
www.gap.com

Fashion Planet
www.fashionplanet.com

Home Shopping Network
www.hsn.com

HMV.com
www.hmv.com

QVC.com
www.qvc.com

Shopping.com
www.shopping.com

Shopping - Malls

These sites list a variety of online stores and offer one-stop shopping.

24HourMall.com
www.24hour-mall.com

Big Planet
www.bpstore.com

Choice Mall
mall.choicemall.com

ChoiceWorld
www.choiceworld.com

Coolshopping
www.coolshopping.com

Ecomall
www.ecomall.com

EZStop Mall
www.ezstopmall.com/homepage.asp

Internet Market
www.internetmarket.org

Family OneStop MegaMall Directory
www.christianonestop.com/
1_mega_mall_directory.htm

SalesHound.com
www.saleshound.com

SkyMall
www.skymall.com

Shopping - Speciality

These sites offer a variety of online stores to choose from.

As Seen On Tv
www.asseenontv.com

AnythingLeftHanded
www.anythingleft-handed.com

eBags.com
www.ebags.com

Electronics NetMall
electronicsnetmall.vstoreelectronics
.com/

FAO Schwarz
www.fao.com

PETsMART.com
www.petsmart.com

PCMall
www.pcmall.com/pcmall

Shoes
www.shoes.com

TechDepot
www.techdepot.com

TechTV Fresh Gear
www.techtv.com/freshgear

TicketMaster
www.ticketmaster.com

Travel

Whether you're looking for accomodation and travel information, adventure, or just a virtual tour, these sites take you there.

Accessible Journeys
www.disabilitytravel.com

Alaska Internet Travel Guide
www.alaskaone.com

Concierge with Conde Nast Traveler
www.concierge.com

GORP.com - Adventure Travel
gorp.com/index.html

Expedia
www.expedia.com

HotWire
www.hotwire.com

Lonely Planet
www.lonelyplanet.com

Photonet.travel
www.photo.net/travel/

RoadsideAmerica
www.roadsideamerica.com

RoughGuides.com
www.roughguides.com/

Travelocity
www.travelocity.com

Virtual Tourist
www.virtualtourist.com/vt

Tutorials - Web & Programming

These sites include free tutorials programming in CGI, HTML or Java to use the Internet.

3D Cafe Tutorials
www.3dcafe.com/asp/tut3ds.asp

DevCentral
devcentral.iftech.com

FindTutorials.com
www.findtutorials.com

Freeskills.com
tutorials.freeskills.com/

Learn the Net
www.learnthenet.com/english/

LearnThat.com
learnthat.com/courses/computer/
htmlintro/

PromotionWorld.com
www.promotionworld.com/tutorial/
000.html

Volunteer Vacations

These sites provide details on how volunteers can participate in programs that are helping people around the world.

Amizade
amizade.org

Cross-Cultural Solutions
www.crossculturalsolutions.org

EarthWatch
www.earthwatch.org

i-to-i - Volunteer, Work & Teach Abroad
www.i-to-i.com

ShortTerm Missions.com
www.shorttermmissions.com

Sousson Foundation
www.sousson.org

The "I Have A Dream" Foundation
www.ihad.org/index.php

Weather

These sites provide up-to-date information on local, regional, and global weather.

Accuweather.com
wwwa.accuweather.com

DisasterLinks.com
www.efwhomesafety.com/onwatch.htm

Intellicast.com
www.intellicast.com

International Weather
www.weatherhub.com

National Hurricane Center
www.nhc.noaa.gov

Net-Cities.com
www.net-cities.com/weather

Weather.com
www.weather.com

Weather Online
www.weatheronline.com

Weather Tracker
www.weather-tracker.com

Wunderground.com
www.wunderground.co

Web Design

These sites provide web design tips for beginners and beyond. Some include examples of award-winning Web design.

BigNoseBird
bignosebird.com

Bigshot Media
www.bigshotmedia.com

Builder.com - Beyond the Code
builder.com.com/

Grantastic Designs
www.grantasticdesigns.com/tips.html

IllusionNewMedia
www.illusionnewmedia.com/
INM_Journey.html

KMGI Studios
www.kmgi.com/

ReallyBig.com
reallybig.com/reallybig.php3

Tripod
www.tripod.lycos.com/build/

Web Design
people2.clarityconnect.com/
webpages5/breaker/des.html

Web Developer's Virtual Library
www.wdvl.com/

Web Style Guide, 2nd edition (Copyright 2002 Patrick J. Lynch and Sarah Horton
www.webstyleguide.com/index.html

Webmonkey - The Developer's Resource
hotwired.lycos.com/webmonkey

WebSpawner.com
www.webspawner.com

Usable Web
usableweb.com

Web Hosting - Free Space

These sites provide Web hosting and free or reasonably priced space.

Brinkster
www.brinkster.com

Crosswinds
www.crosswinds.net

Freeyellow.com
www.freeyellow.com

Freewebspace.net
www.freewebspace.net

GreatNow
www.greatnow.com

HostIndex.com
hostindex.com

Spaceports
www.spaceports.com

Warner Bros: Build a free home page
www2.warnerbros.com/web/hometown

Appendix B: HTML Reference

This appendix contains descriptions of the HTML tags and attributes, and style properties presented in this book.

TABLE 8.1 HTML TAGS AND ATTRIBUTE

Opening Tag	Closing Tag	Attributes	Description
<A>	</A>	NAME= HREF= SRC=	Defines a link and anchor in the same document or in an external file
<ADDRESS>	</ADDRESS>		Places the name or e-mail address of the owner or designer of the Web page
<B>	</B>		Boldfaces text
<BODY>	</BODY>		Defines the body of the Web document
 			Line break
<DEL>	</DEL>		Indicates text deleted from the current version of the document
<EM>	</EM>		Emphasizes text
<FORM>	</FORM>		Creates an interactive form
<FRAME>	</FRAME>	NAME NORESIZE SRC SCROLLING	Sets up contents of frames
<FRAMESET>	</FRAMESET?	ROWS= COLS=	Sets up frames in an HTML document
<H1>...<H6>	</H1>...</H6>		Formats text in headings
<HEAD>	</HEAD>		First section of HTML document
<HR>			Creates a horizontal rule or line
<HTML>	</HTML>		Encloses the entire Web document
<I>	</I>		Italicizes text
<IMG>		SRC= ALT=	Places an image in the document
<INPUT>		TYPE= SIZE= NAME= MAXLENGTH= VALUE=	Specifies input type for interactive forms
<INS>	</INS>		Indicates text inserted into the current version of the document
<LI>			Starts each line of an ordered or unordered list
<META>		NAME= CONTENT=	Placed in head section to identify page to search engines
<NOFRAMES>	</NOFRAMES>		Places text in document for those who can't view frames

TABLE 8.1 HTML TAGS AND ATTRIBUTE

Opening Tag	Closing Tag	Attributes	Description
<OL>	</OL>		Creates an ordered or numbered list
<OPTION>			Identifies each menu item on a form within the <SELECT> tags
<P>	</P>		Starts a new paragraph
<SCRIPT>	</SCRIPT>	TYPE= SRC=	Container used to hold JavaScript
<SELECT>	</SELECT>		Defines a drop-down menu on a form
<STRONG>	</STRONG>		Strongly emphasizes text
<STYLE>	</STYLE>	TYPE=	Defines up styles for the current document
_			Subscripts text
[	]		Superscripts text
<TABLE>	</TABLE>	BORDER CELLSPACING CELLPADDING	Encloses entire table
<TD>	</TD>		Encloses a cell in a table that contains a heading
<TEXTAREA>	</TEXTAREA>	COLS= ROWS=	Defines a text area on a form
<TH>	</TH>		Encloses a cell in a table that contains a heading
<TITLE>	</TITLE>		Must appear in the head section— identifies entire page
<TR>	</TR>		Encloses each row of a table
<UL>	</UL>		Creates an unordered or bulleted list
<!--	-->		Indicates a comment—text placed between these tags is ignored by the Web browser

TABLE 8.2 SOME CSS PROPERTIES

Property	Example	Description
font-family	H1 {font-family: Arial}	Defines the font to be used
font-style	H3 {font-style: italic}	Defines the type of style, such as *normal*, *italic*, or *oblique*
font-size	BODY {font-size: 14 pt}	Sets the size of the text font. Can be measured in values: points (pt), inches (in), centimetres (cm); absolute size: small, x-small, medium, large, x-large, xx-large; relative size: smaller, larger percentage of the parent font size: %
font-weight	P.bold {font-weight: bold}	Defines text weight as normal, bold, bolder, lighter, 100, 200, 300, 400 (being normal), 500, 600, or 700
font-variant	H2 {font-variant: small-caps}	Defines text as normal or small-caps
line-height	P.double {line-height: 18 pt}	Sets the distance between the baselines of two adjacent lines of the same paragraph. Can be set to normal, or measured in points (pt), inches (in), centimeters (cm), pixels (px), or a percentage.
text-indent	P {text-indent: 1.5 in}	Indents the first line of each paragraph by the amount indicated. Measured in points (pt), inches (in), centimeters (cm), or pixels (px).
text-align	H1 {text-align: center}	Determines the alignment of text and can be left, right, center, or justify.
text-transform	H3 {text-transform: capitalize}	Determines the case of text such as none, capitalize, upper case, or lower case.
vertical-align	IMG {vertical-align: middle}	Determines the vertical positioning of the element. Can be set to baseline, sub (subscript), super (superscript), top, text top, middle, bottom, text bottom, or a percentage.
text-decoration	P.strike {text-decoration: line-through}	Determines decorations that are added to text. Can be set to: none, underline, overline, line-through, or blink.

TABLE 8.2 SOME CSS PROPERTIES

Property	Example	Description
color	H2 {color: red}	Sets the color for the tag. Can be set to a common color name ("red"), or the hex value.
background-color	BODY {background-color: #FFFF00}	Defines the background color of an element (can be a color name, hex value, or *transparent*).
background-image	BODY {background-image: url(logo.gif)}	Defines the background image of an element.
background-repeat	BODY {background-image: url(logo.gif); background-repeat: repeat}	Determines how the image is repeated if a background image is specified. A value of *repeat* means that the image is tiled (repeated both horizontally and vertically). Values of repeat-x and repeat-y values repeat the image horizontally or vertically. If set to no repeat, the image is not repeated.
background-attachment	BODY {background-image: url(logo.gif); background-attachment: fixed)}	Determines if a background image is *fixed* with regard to the page, or if it *scroll*s (default) along with the content.
background-position	BODY {background-image: url(logo.gif); background-attachment: fixed; background-position: center-center}	Determines the initial position of a background image, and is specified as a pair of measurements that position the top-left corner of the image at the top-left corner of the window. The position can be entered as a percentage, a length; Or set with a vertical position of top, center, bottom, and a horizontal position of left, center, right.